who do you look like?

JOHN DEVRIES

who do you look like?

A devotional guiding us to look like Jesus

Grand Rapids, Michigan

Who Do You Look Like © 2014 by John DeVries

Project Philip Publishing
4180 44th St. SE Suite A
Grand Rapids, MI 49512

www.projectphilipministries.org

ISBN: 978-0-9884202-3-6

All rights reserved. No part of this book may be reproduced without written permission, except for brief quotations in books and critical reviews.

Unless otherwise noted all Scripture quotations are taken from the *Holy Bible, New Living Translation* (NLT) copyright 1996 by Tyndale House Publishers.

First Printing, 2014

Acknowledgments:
*I gratefully acknowledge the tremendous input
from my wife, Adelaide, who has provided suggestions and
counsel for every meditation in this book.*

Dedication:
*To all who do not know what they really look like and
suffer from feelings of failure and worthlessness.*

Dr. John DeVries is the founder of a Christian non-profit organization called Mission India and a Christian non-profit called Project Philip Ministries. You will notice frequent references to the people of India in this book. You will also sense his deep love for India and his intense desire to see this nation transformed through the new sense of personal value Christ brings when He inhabits us. John invites you to visit the Mission India website at www.missionindia.org. Or you may contact Mission India at (877) 644-6342 or email at info@missionindia.org if you would like to learn more about Mission India. You may also contact Project Philip Ministries on the web or email at info@projectphilipministries.org. This address has listings of evangelistic Bible courses for use in English speaking countries

4180 44th SE Suite A

Grand Rapids, MI 49512-4057

PLEASE READ THIS FIRST!

Who do you look like? Do you look like a wealthy business person? Like a rich farmer? Like a beauty queen? Like a famous athlete? Do you secretly think that maybe you really look like…well, perhaps a wreck? Did it ever occur to you that our looks depend on what is inside, and not on our make-up and lipstick or on our muscles and tattoos. Authentic attractiveness, what we all long for, comes from the beauty that is within.

Did you know that you were made to look like God? That sort of takes your breath away…me…look like God? You have to be kidding! But I'm not kidding. More importantly the Bible isn't kidding. That is exactly what it says in the very first chapter. And God said, "let us make humans in our image and our likeness" (*Genesis 1:26*).

When you discover the truth about yourself, that you were created in God's image, you will have discovered the most transforming concept in the world! The devil is always trying to tell us that we are nothing, nobodies, worthless, ugly, fat or skinny and failures in most areas. Of course, there is a bit of truth in that. The Bible tells us that without God that is what we are! However, Jesus came to restore us to God's image and likeness. Both as God, and as a human, he showed us what a human being is really supposed to look like.

who do you look like?

Now, are you ready for the greatest truth in the world? Jesus told us that if we trusted him, he would, through his Spirit, enter us and live in us to transform us and restore us to resemble him perfectly. Wouldn't you like to look like Jesus? That's what this book is all about. It is about being restored to become the image of Jesus. The truth that Jesus lives in us, is taught over 170 times, in the New Testament. It is the most frequently mentioned truth in the Bible. Here are two well-known statements:

*I have been crucified with Christ,
and I no longer live, but Christ lives <u>in me</u>.*
(Galatians 2:20)

I am the vine; you are the branches. If a man remains in me, and I in him, he will bear much fruit; apart from me you can do nothing.
(John 15:5)

Wouldn't you love to be able to answer the question, Who do you look like? by saying, I look like Jesus? That is possible, and it is about this truth that this book is written.

In the first section of this book, we will introduce the basic truth that when we believe in Christ, he comes into us, dwells in us, and begins to transform us by the power of his Holy Spirit. We are to see ourselves as

PLEASE READ THIS FIRST

being the dwelling place of Jesus. We are his mansions, his temples, his oval offices.

In the second section, we will study who Jesus is. We cannot build our self-image merely on the fact that Jesus lives in us. We need to know who he is and what he has done in creating and then saving the world from sin. We need to know about his love. If we grasp just a little of how great Jesus is, the wonder of his presence through his Spirit in us becomes the most positive, most wonderful, most exciting experience we can have.

In the remaining sections, we will see what Jesus looks like in terms of spiritual qualities such as forgiveness, transformation, love, and a life-giver. If Christ is in us, then these qualities will also shine from us. Love, of course, is the greatest of all of these qualities. An Old Testament prophet describes God's love in these poetic words:

Do not fear, O Zion;
Do not let your hands hang limp.
The Lord your God is with you,
he is mighty to save.
He will take great delight in you,
he will quiet you with his love,
he will rejoice over you with singing.
Zephaniah 3:16

who do you look like?

Picture a mom or dad cuddling a newborn baby and singing softly to her. As soon as the little baby starts responding with a smile and cooing sounds, the parents swell with pride at this little child they have produced in their image and likeness. Jesus describes his relationship with you in the same way. Imagine Jesus saying this to you: *I made you. You resemble me. I created you in my image and in my likeness. Stop comparing yourself to the latest of the culture's choice of the most beautiful woman or most handsome man and feeling that you do not 'measure up' because of your looks. Stop looking at yourself in terms of how much you own, how many people know you, what kind of car you drive, what kind of clothes you wear, or where you live. Look at yourself as I look at you…as the place where I, Jesus, dwell through my Holy Spirit. I delight in you! I am rejoicing over you with singing! I want to quiet you with my love, encourage you with my power, embrace and hold you close.*

To be a follower who trusts in Jesus means that you believe in God's unconditional love for you. Regardless of what a mess you might be in, you never can erase the fact that you are a child of God, created in his image; you are an object of his eternal, unconditional love!

If you believe in Jesus and trust that he loves you

enough to forgive the mess you have made of your life, then he lives in you. Your goal in life is to allow him to shine through you so that through his miraculous, transforming power, he will transform you into his image and likeness. Belonging to Jesus is the divine makeover, which begins in this life and is completed when we enter the next phase of life after death! Read this little book. Try reading a chapter a day. Find out the joy of beginning to look like Jesus and develop an entirely new way of looking at yourself.

Try Floating…

Listening to Jesus is like *floating* on a raft. Think of a nice, warm day with the sun shining brightly. You have a comfortable air mattress, and the lake water is warm. What a day just to float on the raft, letting the breeze and water cool you! Floating is resting. Imagine that a verse of the Bible is your spiritual float; a rubber mattress for the day as you float on water. You get on it by putting it in your mind. Throughout the day you pull it up, you grab it, you look at what is happening to you and interpret it in the light of the verse. What is Jesus saying about this circumstance in the light of the verse?

You will find that as you learn how to float on a verse, you are learning how to listen to Jesus! Prayer will take

who do you look like?

on a whole new dimension. It won't be just you talking—you will be listening to the friend who lives in you as he speaks to you through his Word, the Bible, and shows you how the verse fits the challenges and circumstances you are experiencing that day. If you share these experiences and discoveries with your family, friends, and small group, you (and they) will discover a new excitement and joy in following Jesus. It is very IMPORTANT that you share experiences in listening prayer at each meeting of your small group. You should all be using the same floating verse and encourage each other with the decisions and courage and help the verse gave you.

At the head of each of the six parts of the book you will find a verse, or partial verse to use as your floating verse as you work your way through the chapters in that section. It is best to use the same verse for at least a week or two so that it becomes a vital part of your being.

PLEASE READ THIS FIRST

Contents

Part One: Where are you, Jesus?

Jesus is not out there looking down on us, but, when we believe in him, he is within us, shining out of us! He says, Here I am! I stand at the door and knock. If anyone hears my voice and opens the door, I will come in and eat with him and he with me (Revelation 3:20). We must look at ourselves as being the residences of Jesus Christ, the King of Kings, and we must not build our self-images on our looks or on our money or our fame. We must see ourselves as being the mansions of Jesus, the Lord of the universe, and we must allow him to take over and begin the process of transforming us to look like him. We look like that which is inside us. If Jesus is in us, then we must strive to let his light shine out of us; when it does, we will look like him!

Part Two: Who are you, Jesus? ✓

If the president of the nation were to visit us regularly, our personal sense of value would dramatically increase. Christ is infinitely more important than any other person, and he lives in us. Understanding who Christ is, and that this great being dwells in us, dramatically improves our personal sense of value.

Part Three: Acceptance.

One of the most amazing characteristics of Jesus is his ability to accept us in spite of all the wrong we have done. He demonstrated this by bearing our punishment. His is not a cheap, meaningless forgiveness and acceptance. He paid eternal hell for us in order to forgive us. He makes us as if we have never sinned! We begin to look like Jesus when in his divine, supernatural power, he enables us to accept and forgive even our worst enemies. We cannot do that on our own, but Jesus can enable us to do it. He wants us to look like him. Forgiveness is one of his most wonderful and most powerful attributes.

Part Four: Hope.

Jesus compares our relationship with him to that of a vine and a branch. His life flows into us, transforming us to enable us to love others. He embraced the poor and suffering, the weak and the crippled. He wants us to look like him, doing what he would do. His followers are filled with hope and with joyful anticipation of the many ways his beauty will shine from them. Life has meaning and an exciting new purpose.

Part Five: Friendship.

To look like Jesus requires constant contact with him. This is done in many different ways, not only by talking to him but also by listening to him. It involves taking a thought from the Bible each day and then looking at everything through that thought. The words of the Bible become our spiritual glasses and we see everything that happens in the light of this verse. The Holy Spirit gives a new, spiritual dimension to everything that occurs to us. This is called "listening prayer" and as we discover the new power in listening prayer, our confidence and joy will dramatically increase and the more we pray and listen, the more we will look like Jesus.

Part Six: Love.

Jesus made an awesome prediction one day. He said: *If anyone is thirsty, let him come to me and drink. Whoever believes in me, as the Scripture has said, streams of living water will flow from within him* (John 7:37-38). He was speaking of the Spirit whom those who believed in him were later to receive. When we believe in Jesus and surrender to him, he makes living water (eternal life) flow out of us, into others. There really isn't anything greater for us to be than channels of life that never ends!

Each of these six parts is further divided into short chapters with a few questions and a closing prayer at the end of each chapter. It is my sincere prayer that you may be transformed by finding out that you really can look like—Jesus! In finding that out, I pray that it will become a glorious, increasingly joy-filled, transforming experience that will continue for eternity!

PART ONE

Where Are You, Jesus

Arise, shine, for your light has come, and the glory of the Lord has risen upon you... nations [people] will come to your light.
—Isaiah 60:1, 3

Where Are You, Jesus? Christ is not out there looking down on us; when we believe in him, he is within us, shining out of us! He says, *Look! Here I stand at the door and knock. If you hear me calling and open the door, I will come in, and we will share a meal as friends.* (Revelation 3:20). We must look at ourselves as being the residence of Jesus Christ, the King of Kings, and we must not build our self-images on our looks, our money, or our fame. We must see ourselves as being the mansions of Jesus, the Lord of the universe, and we must allow him to

who do you look like?

take over and begin the process of transforming us to look like him. We look like that which is inside us. If Jesus is in us, then we must strive to let his light shine out of us; when it does, we will look like him!

> Float this verse daily during part One
> ...*but Christ lives in me...* (Galatians 2:20)

Chapter One

Who Do You Look Like?

For the majority of our lives, my wife Adelaide and I have been devoted to our ministry in India. There are 938,000,000 people in India who live on less than $2.50 per day! They are the poorest people in the world. They are called Dalits or untouchables. These people, especially the women, are taught from birth that they are sub-humans with less value than a cow. If they leave their footprint in the sand on a village path and a high-caste person steps on it, the high-caste person believes that he will be polluted and will have to go to the village priest for cleansing. If a Dalit draws water from a high-caste person's well, the people believe that it will take several days to get rid of the spiritual pollution on that well. Dalit girls seldom go to school.

who do you look like?

Even though India's constitution claims all people are equal, that equality is rarely practiced.

Four hundred million of these people cannot read a word, and a total of seven hundred million are unable to read anything more than their names. Can you imagine what they think of themselves? What do they look like to themselves? What image of themselves do they have?

One of Mission India's ministries is to teach these people how to read and write using Bible-based primers. I vividly remember waiting one evening for a literacy class of women to show up to meet our tour group. They had recently learned how to read. I was becoming very impatient, since they were forty-five minutes late, and I wanted to get our group back to the hotel. It was pitch black, and I did not want them to be on the Indian roads at night. The teacher of the literacy class begged me to wait, and so I did.

About an hour later the women showed up, each looking like a queen; they were dressed in the most elegant dresses (saris), and they had beautiful flowers in their hair. I was stunned at how lovely they looked. The teacher whispered to me, *See, Sir, six months ago these women would have come directly from the fields where they had worked all day, dirty and smelly. Now, since they have learned to read and have come to understand how Jesus saves them, they wish first to shower, put on their best clothes, and adorn their hair with flowers. They are so proud of themselves. They are becoming like Jesus, and they have never before known such joy and confidence. You can almost see Jesus in their beauty!*

I stood there with tears running down my face as I listened to them read from the Bible and saw the joy radiating from the smiles on their faces. These women had been taught that they were of less value than cows, but in reality each was an image-bearer of Jesus. Through Christ's presence in them, they now had an entirely new concept of who they were. No longer did they think they were outcastes, but instead they knew that they were image-bearers of the one, true God. They knew that they were princesses, children of the King of the universe!

Ask yourself this question: Who do I look like? You may be unnecessarily walking around with the blues, depressed and letting your hands hang limp! The devil may be whispering to you that you

who do you look like?

are ugly and fat or skinny and homely. You may believe that you look like a failure. Some of it may be true, but you must ask yourself, "How does Jesus see me? What do I look like to him? Is he shining out of me?" It may be that Jesus' answer to this question is radically different than your answer! Many times Christians build their identities and values in the same way that non-Christians do. They base their worth on their possessions and their accomplishments. They are often discouraged and depressed, focusing on their sins and failures. They fail to see the infinite, unlimited power available to them through the indwelling presence of Christ. They forget Christ's great promise found in Ephesians 3:20-21, that Christ, through his power in us, can do things through us that we could never ask or even imagine on our own. Little of what impresses us impresses Jesus. He wants us to look like him; he was far more concerned with the little people of his day than with the leaders, especially the religious leaders who were very hypocritical. He is not impressed with human looks, possessions, or fame. He wants his characteristics of love and concern, especially for others in trouble, to shine from us.

Here are some of the ways in which we look like Jesus. This list is amazing, and if your hands are hanging limp and you feel as if you are an utter failure, remind yourself that because you believe in Jesus and therefore belong to him, this is the way in which Jesus sees you right now. Repeat these statements to yourself and see what happens to the blues.

1. I am a participant in the divine nature. ...*And by that same mighty power, he has given us all of his rich and wonderful promises. He has promised that you will escape the decadence all around you caused by evil desires and that you will share in his divine nature.* (2 Peter 1:4)

2. Christ lives in me! *I myself no longer live, but Christ lives in me. So I live my life in this earthly body by trusting in the Son of God, who loved me and gave himself for me.* (Galatians 2:20).

3. I share in God's authority over <u>principalities and powers </u>(demonic powers). *The seventy-two returned with joy and said, "Lord, even*

who do you look like?

the demons submit to us in your name" (Luke 10:17). (NIV)

4. I am among God's <u>closest relatives</u> and am higher than the angels who were created as ministering servants. *And God said, "let us make man in our image, in our likeness and let them rule…over all the earth"* (Genesis 1:26). (NIV)

5. I will <u>judge the angels</u>. The angels are messengers of God, but they are not his image bearers like I am! *Don't you know that we Christians will judge the angels (1 Corinthians 6:3)? But angels are only servants. They are spirits sent from God to care for those who will receive salvation* (Hebrews 1:14).

6. I am the <u>light of the world</u>. The light of Christ is not shining down on us, but it is in us, shining out of us, and it drives away demonic darkness. *You are the light of the world* (Matthew 5:14).

7. I am a branch of Jesus, he is my vine, and his life flows into me, producing fruit. *Yes, I am the vine; you are the branches. Those who remain in me, and I in them, will produce much fruit.* (John 15:5).

8. I am a fountain of living water (eternal life), which keeps multiplying supernaturally. *Who ever believes in me, as the Scripture has said, streams of living water will flow from within him* (John 7:38) (NIV). *Now unto him who is able to do immeasurably more than all we ask or imagine, according to his power that is at work in us...* (Ephesians 3:20).

9. I am the residence of the King of Kings and Lord of Lords. *Don't you know that all of you together are God's temple and that the Spirit of God lives in you* (1 Corinthians 3:16)?

10. I am putting on the armor of light. *Let us... put on the armor of light* (Romans 13:12) (NIV).

11. I have the <u>uniform and badge of prayer</u>, which binds demonic power. *Whatsoever you bind on earth will be bound in heaven…* (Matthew 18:18) (NIV).

12. I have access to the <u>infinite resources of Jesus</u>. *You didn't choose me. I chose you. I appointed you to go and produce fruit that will last, so that the Father will give you whatever you ask for, using my name. Then the Father will give you whatever you ask in my name* (John 15:16).

The feeling that I lack personal value always results in a bad self-image. This bad self-image robs us of vision, courage, and the ability to tackle life's challenges. Instead of thinking of salvation merely as some future ticket from hell to heaven, we must realize that salvation is the divine power to heal us inwardly at this moment. Salvation makes each of us a new person! We must learn that through the indwelling presence of Christ, we share in Christ's infinite value and purpose. Transformation comes from inside, from a new respect for God's work in us, <u>a work which is occurring right now!</u> While realizing that, in and of ourselves, we have failed, the gift of God, new life in Christ, has made us new people!

Through Jesus' presence in us we have new courage, vision, and confidence. The devil knows what we really look like and wants to keep that a secret from us. His goal is to make us concentrate on our sins and failures and ignore what Christ has made us to be. If he can accomplish that, he knows we will be his prisoners, doomed to sadness and destruction.

Reflect

1. Which of the various ways in which God looks at us affected you the most, and why?

2. How do these concepts transform your belief about your self-image?

3. Just who do you think you are? After reading this, is your image of yourself consistent with who you really are in God's sight? If not, how can you change? Read Chapter Two!

who do you look like?

Prayer

> *Precious Savior, help me to understand who I look like. Come into my life. Transform me to look like you. In your name, I pray. Amen.*

Chapter Two

Where is Jesus?

***Arise*...** Isaiah 60:1(NIV)

I was born twenty-five pounds overweight, a condition from which I have yet to recover! Well, obviously the first part isn't true, but if you'd see me, you'd know that the second part of that sentence is no exaggeration. Because I've always been overweight, I gained the nickname *Fat Stuff* early in life. That nickname, combined with a lack of coordination and athletic ability, did not do much to create a positive self-image.

Consequently I went through life suffering much depression caused by the wrong way of seeing myself. I saw myself, not as being created in the image of Jesus, but as being a complete failure. I was always chosen last for a ball team, because I would insure that the side that chose me would be defeated. As I grew older, I found that my negative self-image and sense of worthlessness was the cause of lingering depression.

I'm sharing this, not because I'm unusual, but rather because everyone suffers to a greater or lesser degree from feelings of failure and worthlessness. None of us seem to be satisfied with our looks; our ears are too big or our nose is too long or we are too tall or too short. We seldom feel that we have enough money or possessions. We are never satisfied!

Worldwide, people have very serious problems with feelings of worthlessness. Some people have been abused emotionally or sexually by parents, relatives, or friends, with resulting feelings of worthlessness, poor self-image, and lack of purpose. One of the reasons for alcoholism and drug abuse is our failure to be able to look at ourselves. We need an escape, and too often we look for it in drugs and alcohol. Feelings of insignificance, a poor self-image, and no purpose in life are far more common than we realize. They exist in every country, among all people.

I remember an Indian pastor crying during a prayer time with a team of American pastors I had taken there. When the prayer was over, he apologized, saying that as we prayed he had been attacked by Satan. He had been an untouchable (a Dalit), and the devil accused him of pride. *How can you, an untouchable, place yourself on the same level as these Americans?* the devil taunted. *You have no right to be praying with Americans! You are an untouchable! You are worth less than a cow*! Then suddenly the Holy Spirit reminded him of who he REALLY was, namely, a child of the King who had royal blood spilled over him. He received a new sense of self-worth and dignity, and this brought a new smile to his face. His self-image and his purpose in life were restored because of Christ who lived in him.

We all long to step out of the shadows into the light, but we don't know how. We keep looking at ourselves, trying to overcome our failures and improve our appearance, but it doesn't work. No matter how much fame or money or power we get, these things only help us to temporarily feel positive about ourselves, at best.

who do you look like?

There is another way to build a good self-image and gain a satisfying sense of value. That's what this book is all about. Being born again is more than getting a ticket which saves you from going to hell and gets you into heaven after you die. It is true that people who are born again won't go to hell, but that's only part of the meaning of being born again. Being born again isn't some magical ticket, but it is an inner transformation. The Bible says it is being made new. *If anyone is in Christ, he is a new creation, the old has gone, and the new has come* (2 Corinthians 5:17 NIV). This verse is translated in the New Living Translation as: *What this means is that those who become Christians become new persons. They are not the same anymore, for the old life is gone; the new life has begun!*

Being born again means that we are in Christ. This little devotional is intended to help build a new self-image by focusing on the Jesus who lives in us rather than on our physical attractiveness, or our money, or what others say about us. When we discover the One who is in us, when we discover his importance, his power, his beauty, his light and life, then we will not only have a NEW sense of value and a NEW self-image, but we'll also have a NEW sense of purpose and meaning in life. We will go from gloom to joy!

Reflect

1. How does the first picture illustrate the way many people feel, and how does the second express how we would like to feel?

2. What are some of the things that happen to people which destroy their sense of self-value?

3. When do people feel they have no purpose in life?

4. What are some of the most common ways in which most people try to establish a sense of personal value? Why don't these work?

who do you look like?

Prayer

> *Lord, today help me step out of the gloom and into your light; let your light shine out of me. For your sake, Jesus. Amen.*

Chapter Three

Jesus, the Light Is In Us

Arise, Shine... Isaiah 60:1(NIV)

When I found this picture, I fell in love with it. I've shared it with many people since who have had the same reaction to it. When I ask, *What do you like about this picture?*, the answer is always the same. They like the light. Then I ask, *What do you like about the light?* Answers range from liking the glow, the warmth, and the welcoming nature of the light to the fact that the light invites them to the house. If they were out walking, they say that they would not hesitate to go up to this house, but if there were no light streaming from the house, they say that they would be fearful. Unfriendly people might inhabit that house. The streaming light tells us something about the occupants. It attracts us.

Jesus tells us that we are his houses. He stands at the door and knocks. He will come in and live with anyone who opens the door (Revelation 3:20). He is the light of the world, and when he comes in, he lights up our house and our whole yard; our whole demeanor, lit up with his light, makes us to be the light of the world! When Christ comes into someone, he radically transforms that person to have all the winsome attributes you see in the picture of this house. It speaks of warmth, a family, light in darkness… think of all the things that this picture symbolizes.

Light has many functions. Among its many functions I would list these:

Light destroys darkness. A hundred years ago, on a very dark night, a little boy was watching a lamp lighter come down the street when his mom asked him what he was doing. He replied that he was watching a man punch holes in the darkness. Darkness cannot withstand light. Jesus punches holes in our darkness, letting his light shine in and showing us who we really are, namely, his image-bearers, and then letting his light shine out of us.

Light shows the path. The light from this house shows us the way to the house. Whenever there is light, we can see the way, the path. Jesus, as the light of the world, shatters the darkness and illuminates the way to the Father. As he shines out of us we then are a light pointing to the Father of all.

Light shows beauty. Any photographer or artist knows the importance of light in a photograph or painting. Light, carefully applied, makes a picture come to life; it reveals its hidden beauty. When Christ comes in, his light transforms us from the inside out.

Light lifts emotions. In the area in which I live, we once had a period of forty-four consecutive days of rain and thirteen days in which there was no sunshine at all. Because of our frequent rain, folks

who do you look like?

living around here appreciate a sunny day more than others might, and emotions soar when the sun finally shines. As the light of Christ shines from our eyes and smiles and kind words, we become spreaders of joy.

Light gives life. Finally, light and life are inseparably linked together. House plants lean toward the light. Hot houses that are lighted 24/7 grow amazingly lush plants. Light gives life. As Christ shines from within us people, like plants, are inclined to lean toward Jesus!

As we look at this house, there is something more to its light. It is a symbol of two important things: it is a symbol of life and of love. The house is occupied and seems warm and inviting; it is a symbol of love. Welcoming people must live here, loving people.

This picture has helped me imagine what I must look like, since I have been born again. To be born again means this: *I have been crucified with Christ and I no longer live, but Christ lives in me* (Galatians 2:20). I remember the first time this truth dawned on me. I was reading Psalm 27:1, *The Lord is my light…* I could not get beyond that phrase, and a

JESUS THE LIGHT IS IN US

question kept popping up in my mind. *Where is the light, John? Where is the light?* I kept answering, saying, *The light is out there, shining down on me.* Finally, I realized that the light was not outside of me, shining down on me, but rather that it was in me, shining out of me. When I saw that, I thought, *I must stop kicking myself around. The "light of the world" is in me, and that gives me tremendous value!* My value doesn't come from my appearance any more than that house in the picture is attractive because of its architecture. It's the light—the light shining from within me—that's what matters. Every person who believes in Jesus has the light of Jesus inside him. We look like little houses with that warm, inviting light glowing from our eyes, our words, our deeds.

Suddenly God gave me a tool to begin to rebuild that poor self-image, that self-centered drive for perfectionism. *Fat Stuff* died! He was crucified with Christ, and all my sin was removed from my account and paid for by his precious blood. Jesus claimed to be the light of the world, and the light of the world had moved into me! That's what I now look like! I gained a totally new way of looking at myself. That's

who do you look like?

what I want to share with you, with the hope that you will discover the new you, the transformation that being born again brings right now.

Reflect
1. What do you like about the picture of the house?
2. What are five functions of light?
3. What are the two symbols of light as shown in this picture?
4. How is this picture a picture of 2 Corinthians 5:17?

Prayer

> *Savior, help me not to look at myself in terms of my works, or my deeds, or my physical attractiveness or lack of it. Holy Spirit, help me to see Christ living in me. For your sake, I pray, Jesus. Amen.*

Chapter Four

Jesus, the Light Shines Out of Us and When the Light Shines Out of Us, We Look Like Him!

Arise, shine, for your light has come… Isaiah 60:1 (NIV)

One of the most famous and well-loved verses of the Bible is John 3:16 (NIV). *For God loved the world so much he gave his one and only Son that whoever believes in him should not perish but have eternal life.* What is this eternal life about which Jesus speaks? Is it something that happens only when our bodies die? Or is eternal life something which starts now? We must be able to answer this question in order to build a new sense of value and a new self-image on the basis of having Christ in us, rather than on what we think we look like or what we have done. Most of us think of eternal life as something which starts after death.

The Bible teaches us that eternal life starts now. It is placed in us when we first believe in Christ. This is the implication that Paul gives when he describes himself in these words: *I have been crucified with Chris: and I myself no longer live, but Christ lives in me* (Galatians 2:20) (NIV). He does not speak in a future tense. He does not say, *When I die, then I will live forever.* Rather he says he has died already. He claims he was crucified with Christ. That old, worn out wreck that Paul thought he was, was dead.

But what does he mean? What was crucified? Let's call it the old self—the sinful self. The sinful self is the one whose life is based on the principle of living to get. That controlling principle is dead, because we are now filled with Christ. *Fat Stuff* doesn't live anymore. He is done. When I discovered that Christ lived in me, I did not need to have good looks or athletic ability to feel good about myself. The greatest being in the universe, Jesus Christ, lives in me! What matters is that Christ lives in me now, and that he uses me to reveal himself to the world. I have a completely new value, a completely new purpose in life. I am Christ's dwelling place, his sanctuary, his temple.

How does this work? How is Christ in me? Jesus uses the illustration of a vine and a branch found in John 15:1 to help us understand. Our relationship is so close to Christ that he compares it to that of a vine and a branch. Just like the vine brings life to the branch, and, in a sense, the branch is in the vine and the vine is in the branch, so we are bonded to Jesus. We become new, fruitful, productive, transformed people.

Three young men were racing through a train station, and in their haste to make the train, one of them tripped over a box of apples that a poor blind boy was selling, scattering the apples all over the floor. One of the men stopped and started to pick up the apples. The other two said, *Come on, don't stop, we will miss our train. If we miss it, we will have to stay here all night. Let's go!* The third one said, *You guys hurry on. I'm going to pick up these apples for this boy.* The two argued with him, but seeing that

who do you look like?

they couldn't convince the third fellow to leave, they hurried on to catch the train. The third young man remained and, even though he had to wait another day to catch the train, he quietly picked up the apples, put them in the box, and gave the blind boy some money. When he told the boy that all the apples were back in the box, the little blind boy responded by saying, *Mister, who are you? You look like Jesus to me*. Even though he was physically blind, he still could *see* Jesus in the young man who selflessly gave up his entire day to help. Do we look like we have the light in us? Is that what you want to look like?

This new life is light. And the light is the power to give. Jesus is the divine, transforming power which changes us from darkness to light, from getting to giving. Jesus laid aside all his glory and humbled himself to become a man. God gave everything for us, even paying the punishment of hell for us. He put us before himself. That is the supreme power. It is the power to put others before ourselves. Just as the life in the vine enables the branches to produce (and give) fruit, so the life of Christ in us enables us to live for the purpose of giving good things to others and not for getting as much as we can for ourselves.

In John 9:5 Jesus said, *But while I am in the world, I am the light of the world.* He qualified the statement, *I am the light of the world,* when he said that he was the light of the world *only as long as he was in the world,* in his human nature. Christ is in the world in a totally different way now than he was when he lived in Palestine. Christ is now in the world by being in every one of his disciples through his Holy Spirit. This allows him to say of us, *You are the light of the world* (Matthew 5:14). We are the light, not in our power, but in his power. We are connected to the power source. Just as the house in our picture would have no light without its connection to electricity, so we would have no light without the connection of faith to Jesus Christ.

Each day upon arising we should remind ourselves of who it is we want to look like and ask him by his power in us, to make us look more like him each day! That means that we are more interested in helping and giving to others than we are in serving and getting for ourselves.

who do you look like?

Reflect

1. What does Jesus' resurrection mean (1 Corinthians 15:35-58)?

2. When does eternal life start (Galatians 2:20)?

3. How does eternal life flow into us (John 15:1-5)?

4. What do you think *abiding* or *remaining in Christ* means (John 15:7)?

5. What promise is given to those who remain in Christ (John 15:7)?

6. What is the purpose of remaining in Christ (John 15:8)?

Prayer

Savior, these thoughts are difficult to understand. Help me to think of life flowing through the vine into the branch as I think of my relationship to you. Help me to think of electricity flowing into that house making the light shine as I remember you flowing into me and letting your light shine through me. May others see that your light has come, and that it is in me and shining out of me. For your sake, I pray. Amen.

Chapter Five

How Do We Let the Light Shine Out of Us?

*Arise, shine, for your light
has come and the glory of the Lord
will rise upon you. Isaiah 60:1(NIV)*

What is the glory of the Lord? What is this beautiful thing that will rise in us and shine out of us? It is love, love expressed in selfless sacrifice. It is generous love, giving love. It is the love which the Father has lavished on us (I John 3:1), meaning that he gives so generously that it spills out over everything.

We must never think of the glory of the Lord as merely being his power, although it is certainly that.

HOW DO YOU LET THE LIGHT SHINE OUT OF US?

The height of God's beauty is love. God used the sin in the world as the occasion to show the greatest possible expression of love. *But God showed his great love for us by sending Christ to die for us while we were still sinners* (Romans 5:8).

Paul says that we all find it hard to give up our life for a good person but that it is virtually unheard of for one to give up his life for an enemy. But while we were enemies of God, and while we were rebelling against him through our selfishness, Jesus did precisely that; he died for us.

Think of what a miser looks like. If we live merely for ourselves, we will look like (and we will be) misers. No one can get along with a miser unless he is willing to give everything to that selfish person and get nothing in return. God certainly doesn't look like a miser! God gave the life of his Son for us. God is the most generous being in the universe. Jesus is the model of generosity.

Here's what Jesus looks like. Think of yourself the way Christ Jesus thought of himself (Philippians 2:4ff). He had equal status with God, but he didn't think so much of himself that he had to cling to the

who do you look like?

advantages of that status. Not at all. When the time came, he set aside the privileges of deity (of being God) and took on the status of a slave; he became human! Having become human, he stayed human. It was an incredibly humbling process. He didn't claim special privileges. Instead, he lived a selfless, obedient life, and then he died a selfless, obedient death—and the worst kind of death at that: a crucifixion.

Because of that obedience, God lifted him high and honored him far beyond anyone or anything, ever, so that all created beings in heaven and on earth—even those long ago dead and buried—will bow in worship before this Jesus Christ and will call out in praise that he is the master of all, to the glorious honor of God the Father (Philippians 2: 6-11, The Message).

One Thanksgiving Day I had a strange vision as I was driving through one of our many apple orchards. I saw a picture in my mind of an apple tree that kept all its apples stacked in a pyramid around its trunk. I heard it pray, *Thank you, Lord, for allowing me to keep all my apples. I cannot believe how blessed I am. Look at all the other trees. Not only don't they have any apples now, but they also don't even have any leaves. Look at how beautiful my apples are as I have stacked them around my trunk. Thank you, Jesus, for giving me so much. I don't understand why all these other trees don't have as many apples as I have.*

Then I heard God crying as he said, *My precious apple tree, what made you think I created you to keep all your apples? I created you to give them away. The function of an apple tree is not to keep its apples but to bless others by producing apples and giving them away. You have destroyed my purpose for you, and even now the maggots are eating the fruit and soon will be entering your trunk to destroy you.* God measures our worth not by how many apples we keep, but by how many we give away.

The light that dwells in us and flows from us shines in our concern for the sick, the poor, the prisoners, the helpless, and the forgotten ones. It is turned on through our love and concern for the least of the people. This is the fruit that God expects us to produce, and it is the evidence that Christ lives in us. God's glory is seen not in how high and exalted he is, but in how low he stoops to demonstrate his love and concern for us. Jesus never measures by earthly standards. God doesn't think like we think or work like we work. He is no more impressed with how rich you are than he is with an apple tree which keeps its apples. He measures our worth not by how much we get, but by how much we give.

The mark of true followers of Jesus is found not in how high they can climb, but in how low they can reach down to give to others. The more we exalt ourselves, the more we diminish the picture of Christ in us. The more we try to build the picture of what we look like on what we do, how we look, how much money we have, or on our reputations, the more we prevent the light of Christ from shining from us. The beauty of Jesus, which we long to have seen in us, is found in our concern for the fatherless and the widows (James 1:27).

Reflect

1. For what purpose did Christ come according to Luke 4:16-19?
2. Why was Sodom destroyed (Ezekiel 16:49-50)? What does that mean for our wealth?

3. What aspects of Christ's glory (beauty) are described in Philippians 2:6-11?
4. What is the value of one lost person, according to Matthew 18:10-14?

Prayer

> *Savior, help me to see that the beauty and light that are the most important to you are found in my concern for the forgotten and the lost. Grant that I may not seek to climb to the heights, but rather that I may be willing to join you in giving to reach the lowest of the low. May your light shine through my concern for the hurting and hungry people around me. For your sake I pray. Amen.*

Chapter Six

Christ's Light Shining Out of You Will Attract Others

Arise, shine, for your light has come and the glory of the Lord is risen upon you…and nations (people) will come to your light.
Isaiah 60:1, 39 (NIV)

We are back where we started, looking at the light streaming from this house. Remember, it's the light, not the lines of the house, which attract us. What is true for this house—that the light from within is that which attracts others—is also true for each disciple of Jesus. It is not our physical

CHRIST'S LIGHT SHINING OUT OF YOU

beauty (although we should always be neat) which attracts others. Sometimes we can dress and adorn ourselves in such a way that people cannot possibly see Jesus in us! It is not our position, nor our possessions, nor our success by worldly standards that is to be what we look like to others. It's the light of Jesus within us, shining out of us, with all its beckoning warmth that is to be our image.

Remember, there are two requirements for the light to shine. The first one, as you look at this picture of the house, is the fact that the house must be wired and connected to the power supply. When storms come and the power supply is interrupted, the lights go out. We need always to be connected to Christ. In John 15, Christ gives us the command to abide in him, and then he will abide in us. Paul explains what this means in Galatians 2:20 when he says, *I myself no longer live, but Christ lives in me. So I live my life in this earthly body by trusting in the Son of God, who loved me and gave himself for me.* When Paul says he is living by faith, he means that he is living by looking to Jesus and trusting him, not looking to himself or trying to acquire things for himself. Jesus Christ is our power connection.

who do you look like?

It is not enough merely to be connected to the power by trusting Jesus. We must also turn on the lights, by turning the switch to on. The on position which allows the light of Christ to flow into us and out of us is spelled *GIVE*. The off position is spelled *GET*. Each time we are selfish, we turn off the light of Christ. We must give ourselves to Christ in the sense that we allow him to penetrate every part of our being with his spirit of generosity.

A new sense of value comes from seeing the importance of the One living in us. We will look at the importance of Jesus next, and based on his importance, we can start to build and experience a new attitude toward ourselves. These two experiences, of having both value and a positive self-image, will result in our gaining a new purpose in life. Our new purpose can be summarized in the functions of light, as we saw earlier.

<u>Light destroys darkness</u>. Our new mission and purpose in life is to destroy darkness!

<u>Light shows the way to the Father</u>. This is our new task, to tell others about Jesus and thus point all to the Father!

<u>Light reveals beauty</u>. Our whole purpose is to radiate the generous, loving, beautiful concern of the Father for the people who feel smallest in the world.

<u>Light lifts emotions</u>. The Savior comforts others through our words, our deeds, and our love.

<u>Light brings life</u>. More than all else, this is our highest calling. We are life-givers to those who are spiritually dead.

There is no room for us to feel miserable about ourselves if we are born again. Being born again is not first of all, a ticket to heaven, but it is a transformation from darkness to light, RIGHT NOW!

Reflect
1. What are the two requirements for the light to shine from a house?

2. How are these two requirements similar to the two requirements for Christ's light to shine from within us?

3. What was Paul's power connection, according to the second part of Galatians 2:20?

who do you look like?

4. What is the spiritual off switch which keeps the light of Christ from flowing out of us?

5. What is the on switch?

Prayer

> *Savior, thank you for showing me a new, transformed way of living. Help me to discover the new person you have created in me and to live with my mind fixed on you. In your name I pray. Amen.*

PART TWO

Who Are You, Jesus?

Who Are You, Jesus? If the president of the nation were to visit us regularly, our personal sense of value would dramatically increase. Christ is infinitely more important than any other person, and he lives in us. Understanding who Jesus is will determine who we look like. If we don't know who Jesus is, how can we look like him? Understanding that he is the greatest being in the universe, and that this King of Kings dwells in us, will have a great impact on who it is we actually look like!

who do you look like?

FLOAT THIS VERSE DURING PART TWO
Do not fear…do not let your hands hang limp!
Zephaniah 3:16 (NIV)

Chapter Seven

Jesus, the Ruler of the Nations Lives in Us

Think of two buildings. One is the White House with the Oval Office of the president of the United States. The other is Mt. Vernon, George Washington's estate. Which one of these is the most important building? Which one would a terrorist choose to destroy? Not much of a choice, is it? It would be the White House. Why? Is it because the White House is more beautiful than Mount Vernon? Hardly. The importance of the White House comes from the person who lives in it. Mt. Vernon doesn't have an occupant, and hence is only a museum. It has great value, of course, but it is far less significant than the White House. One of the most important offices in the world is the office of the president of the United States. Meeting in this office with his advisors, he makes decisions that affect not only

who do you look like?

the citizens of the United States but also people in other nations as well. The White House gains its importance from more than its looks, or history, or furnishings. The real value of this building comes from the person who occupies it, the President of the United States!

Can you imagine visiting this office? Can you imagine sitting in on some of the morning briefings? Can you imagine that the president of the United States would actually invite you to come, perhaps monthly or weekly, to listen to your views and your requests?

If he did, how would you feel? Like this?

Of course not! You would feel like this!

Every one of us would have a profound new sense of importance! Our whole self-image would be transformed. Feelings of failure would be gone. We would have a tremendous sense of purpose.

Now imagine something even stranger. Imagine that the president did not invite you to his office, but rather invited himself to your house. Imagine that he asked you if he could come to your house to visit you, to use your office. That's so far-fetched it is difficult even to imagine.

However, there is someone knocking on your door. Every day when you get up, that someone knocks. Have you ever wondered who that person is? It is someone far more important than any per-

who do you look like?

son on earth. It is Jesus Christ. One of the reasons we don't know who we are is because we spend so little time thinking about who he is! It is easy to understand how we could feel a sense of importance from being with the president. Doesn't it make sense that if someone far more important than the president wants to come into our lives and live IN us, that should give us a totally new self-image? When we say we are Christians, but we feel like we are failures, we are saying that the One who lives in us really doesn't matter! It would be like saying that it would not matter if the president or prime minister were regularly to come to our house.

Just who is Jesus? How important is he? We will be answering that question as we review the five descriptions of Jesus which we find given in John 1:1-4.

- Christ in us—the way to God.
- Christ in us—the greatness of God.
- Christ in us—the knowledge of God.
- Christ in us—the creating God.
- Christ in us—the life-giving God.

Reflect

1. In what way is the president's office one of the most important offices in the world?

2. What would happen to your sense of value, your self-image, and your purpose in life if you were invited to this office each week?

3. Why would being in this office weekly make you feel important?

4. Is there anyone greater and more powerful than the people who fill this office?

5. Where does that Person want to be, according to Revelation 3:20, and how would you let Him in?

who do you look like?

Prayer

> *Dear Jesus, help me to remember who you are. Guide me as I reflect on your importance and make me see the tremendous honor of having you, through your Holy Spirit, live in me. For your sake, Jesus, I ask this. Amen.*

Chapter Eight

Jesus, the Only Way to God, Lives in Us

In the beginning was the Word…
John 1:1

Did you ever hear the story of the drunk who was asked directions? The man stumbled and stuttered as he tried to describe how to get there. Finally, in frustration and feeling a complete failure, he said, *I guess you can't get there from here.*

All of us get lost from time to time. Men have a very hard time stopping to ask for directions when they are lost. They would much rather continue to go 'round and round' than to be humiliated by having to stop somewhere to ask which way is the right way. My wife is fond of reminding me of that. Get-

who do you look like?

ting lost, for all of us, however, is frustrating, and we feel secure only when we know the way. Jesus came to show us the way to the one true God. He is the ultimate guide. He is the final word on how to get into God's presence. In order to understand the importance of Christ, we need to understand what it means to call Jesus the Word of God. Words have two functions. They can be easily remembered by two words starting with the letter "r": reveal and relate. Words reveal and then relate us to each other.

Although we have been married for many decades, my wife still asks what I am thinking when I am silent for long periods. Although she is my life's partner, she still cannot read my mind. I must speak in order for her to understand what is going on in my head, and if I refuse to talk, she doesn't know what I am thinking. My mind is hidden from her until I use words to tell her my thoughts. She can tell my moods by looking at my face, the stoop of my shoulders, or by seeing if my hands are hanging. She can see if I am happy by my smile, but she cannot see what I am thinking. I have to share that by talking, by using words.

Words are necessary to reveal to others who we are. In this sinful world we can lie and thus disguise who we are. The Bible tells us that Satan is the father of all lies. He uses words to hide himself. But there is no shadow of deceit with God. And, wonder of wonders, God chooses words to reveal himself to us! That Word is Jesus, the second Person of the Trinity. He is God's Word to us, and thus, he becomes the way for us to the Father. Jesus said, *I am the way, the truth, and the life. No one can come to the Father except through me* (John 14:6).

How important is that function of being the WAY to the Father? The world lives in darkness, wondering who God is. People create idols of wood and stone and bow down to worship lifeless gods. They live in darkness, fear, and superstition. How valuable is it to know the true, loving, perfect God? Knowing the truth about God is the single most valuable treasure we can possess. Now think that the One who reveals God is knocking on your door, asking to come in and eat with you every day

who do you look like?

(Revelation 3:20)! How does the fact that the most important person in the world is knocking at the door of your heart right now, asking you to let him in, affect you? If Jesus is so important, doesn't his presence in you give you a new feeling of importance?

The second function of words is to relate us to one another. A most debilitating handicap is to be severely impaired in the areas of speech and hearing, for that cuts one off from all contact. To be unable to hear or speak can cause great loneliness. Words are bridges on which relationships are built. The Word of God, Jesus, in revealing who the Father is, builds many kinds of relationships with the Father for us. Here are some of them. He puts us in these relationships when he comes into us to live in us. *If anyone is IN Christ he is a new creation, the old is gone, the new has come!* (2 Corinthians 5:17 (NIV)). The New Living Translation states this verse this way: *What this means is that those who become Christians become new persons. They are not the same anymore, for the old life is gone. A new life has begun!* To be in Christ is to live a new life.

1. <u>It is to be in a relationship like a branch is to the vine</u>. *Yes, I am the vine; you are the branches* (John 15:5).
2. <u>It is to be God's closest relative!</u> *Behold, what manner of love the Father has lavished on us that we should be called children of God and such we are* (1 John 3:1) (NIV)
3. <u>It is to be God's heirs.</u> *And since we are his children, we will share his treasures—for everything God gives to his Son, Christ, is ours too. But if we are to share his glory, we must also share his suffering.* (Romans 8:17).
4. <u>It is to be in, or a member of, the body of Christ.</u> *Now all of you together are Christ's body, and each one of you is a separate and necessary part of it* (1 Corinthians 12:27).
5. <u>It is to have our name "tattooed" on the palms of God's hands.</u> *See, I have written your name on (the palms of) my hand* (Isaiah 49:16). God loves us so much that he has our names engraved on the palms of his hands!

How important do you think this person is who not only reveals to us the true nature of God the Father, but who also becomes the way to enter this

who do you look like?

multifaceted relationship with the Father? This little survey of Bible verses reveals the depth there is to our relationship with the Father through Jesus, a far deeper and more profound relationship than any other relationship. Remember, it is a relationship with the GREATEST, MOST IMPORTANT BEING IN THE UNIVERSE! Because Christ is in us, we are as close to Jesus as a branch is to its vine. We are called the children of God, his heirs, and we are called a part of Christ's body. Our names are engraved on his hands.

Yes, you would feel pretty important if the president of the USA came to your house. What if he came to live with you? Jesus is infinitely greater than any other person who has ever lived, and he wants to live in you. He is the Word of God—the One who shows us the way into eternal life. He is the One who shows by his words that the Father in heaven loves us unconditionally and lavishes that love on us. He has promised that he, the Word, the revelation of the right and only way to the Father, will come, create new life in us and dwell in us forever. Accept that offer now.

Reflect
1. What are the two functions of words? How does Jesus "the Word made flesh" fulfill this function?
2. Since words are the foundation of all relationships, and Christ is the Word of God, then he becomes the foundation of our relationship with God. According to Revelation 3:20, what is Jesus doing to establish our relationship with God.
3. The list of five verses listed above highlights the depth of our new relationship with God. Which one of these five verses particularly encourages you today?

Prayer

> *Dear Jesus, please forgive me for not paying attention and for failing to appreciate not only who you are, but where you are. I ask you again, Lord Jesus, come into my heart and come in to stay here with me throughout all my life on earth, and then for eternity with you. Enable me to love you above all, for I ask it in your name, Jesus. Amen.*

Chapter Nine

Jesus the Creator-Redeemer of the Universe...

Lives in Us...

In the beginning the Word already existed. He was with God, and he (the Word) was God…
John 1:1

Who is this One who stands at the door of our hearts? Who wants to come in and dwell with us? How great is he? How important is he? He is the Way. He knows the way, because he is the Way. Everyone searches for the way to immortality. Christ claims he is the only way. One third of the world's people follow him. But he is more than merely the Way. Christ's greatness is shown in two more ways. It is shown in how high and how exalted he is, and it is shown in how he humbles himself.

The greatness and the exaltedness of God is shown in God's address to Job. Read Job 1 and 2. Think you have problems? Look at this mysterious man. Job, however, never blamed God; nevertheless, God did not immediately remove Job's problems. He merely impressed on Job how high and how powerful he is.

> ² *"Who is this that questions my wisdom*
> *with such ignorant words?*
> ³ *Brace yourself like a man,*
> *because I have some questions for you,*
> *and you must answer them.*
> ⁴ *"Where were you when I laid the foundations*
> *of the earth?*
> *Tell me, if you know so much.*
> ⁵ *Who determined its dimensions*
> *and stretched out the surveying line?*
> ⁶ *What supports its foundations,*
> *and who laid its cornerstone*
> ⁷ *as the morning stars sang together*
> *and all the angels shouted for joy?*

who do you look like?

*^{8} "Who kept the sea inside its boundaries
as it burst from the womb,
^{9} and as I clothed it with clouds
and wrapped it in thick darkness?
^{10} For I locked it behind barred gates,
limiting its shores.
^{11} I said, 'This far and no farther will you come.
Here your proud waves must stop!'
^{12} "Have you ever commanded
the morning to appear
and caused the dawn to rise in the east?
Job 38:2-12*

This passage deserves careful, slow, meditative reading. God is so high, so majestic, and so far beyond us. Consider those questions God asked Job, since he is also asking them of us. Where were we when he created the world and all the angels shouted for joy? Did he consult with us to find out how big and how wide and how wonderful all this should be? Of course he did not! Who is knocking at our door each morning, wanting to come into us? It is this God, this great, awesome God. He wants to come into us spiritually through his Holy Spirit.

How are we honoring him by the way we look at ourselves? When we think we are nothing, we are saying he doesn't matter! Is it nothing to have the Creator God live in us? Is there nothing in this God that is exciting enough to pull us out of our sense of failure, when we feel we are worthless and nothing? Does his love mean nothing to us? Does not his greatness give us a sense of importance?

There is another aspect to his greatness, and it is expressed in Philippians 2:6-8:

> *Though he was God, he did not demand*
> *and cling to his rights as God.*
> *He made himself nothing;*
> *He took the humble position of a slave*
> *and appeared in human form.*
> *And in human form he obediently*
> *humbled himself even further*
> *by dying a criminal's death on the cross.*
> *Because of this, God raised him up*
> *to the heights of heaven*
> *and gave him a name that is above*
> *every other name,*
> *so that at the name of Jesus*

who do you look like?

*every knee will bow
in heaven and on earth and under the earth
and every tongue will confess that
Jesus Christ is Lord
to the glory of God the Father.*

If you think it is hard to fathom God's greatness as expressed in Job 38, then think of God's love. God's true greatness is expressed in his awesome love, a love that enabled Christ to leave the glories of heaven and to limit himself to time and to our human nature. Christ became a human, while still remaining God. Who can comprehend this? God is so great that his love penetrates to the deepest and the lowest levels. He comes riding not in a great chariot, but on the colt of a donkey! He comes not in majesty, but in excruciating suffering and pain, dying an eternal death on Calvary's cross to pay for our sins.

Is it nothing that this amazing Jesus literally stands before us each day, longing to come into us and live in us? Is his love and sacrifice so insignificant that it makes no difference in how we feel about ourselves? Yes, we have failed, and we have sinned! But he loves us anyway—and our value comes not from ourselves, but from the fact that the greatest Being, the One who stooped so low as to enter hell for us, now loves us so much that he longs to live within us!

Jesus is so great that his love penetrates to the darkest and lowest levels of our lives. He doesn't ride in great processions in a fancy black Cadillac, but rather, he rode on the colt of a donkey. He came to us not in majesty but in excruciating suffering and pain, dying an eternal death on Calvary's cross to pay for our sins.

What does it mean to be loved this much by the majestic Creator-Redeemer? Listen to these words from his servant John: *In the beginning the Word already existed. He was with God, and he was God. He was in the beginning with God. He created everything there is. Nothing exists that he didn't make. Life itself was in him, and this life gives light to everyone. The light shines through the darkness, and the darkness can never extinguish it.* (John 1:1-4). Imagine that that person lives in you. Better still, KNOW that that person lives in you, because you trust in him!

who do you look like?

Reflect

1. List ways in which God shows his greatness in nature (Job 38:2-12).

2. List the ways in which God's greatness is shown in his ability to *come down* as reflected in Philippians 2:6-8.

3. Which of these two forms of greatness is the *greatest*? Which one does Christ want to reveal through you by his presence in you according to Matthew 25:40?

Prayer

> *Precious Savior, Forgive me for failing so often to see this double greatness—that you are both Creator and Redeemer. I am humbled and in awe to think that you love me so much that you are willing to live in me, to make me your temple! Thank you, Jesus!!!*
> *Amen.*

Chapter Ten

Jesus, the One Who Is in God the Father... Lives in Us!

The Father and I are one. John 10:30
Anyone who has seen me has seen the Father!
John 14:9

It was about noon on the day that I suddenly lost the sight in my left eye. I looked up, and there was a gray shadow blocking my vision. I covered my right eye and found that I could not see through my left eye at all. I had suddenly and mysteriously gone blind in one eye.

In the following days, the doctors I saw were not encouraging. They said that in some unknown way, the blood flow to my left eye had been blocked

who do you look like?

and I would never regain my sight. I certainly had not planned on losing my sight! It was a giant surprise to me, but it was no surprise to the One living in me, for he is timeless and omniscient. He has no beginning and no end. He lives outside of time. Everything is the present for him. He knew the precise moment my sight would be taken away. We cannot understand eternity, for we are creatures of time, bound and locked out of the present; hurling onward between the past and the future. Jesus lives in an eternal present. Forgetting much of the past and knowing nothing of the future, we seem always to be surprised by current events, just as I was surprised by the loss of the sight in my eye. Jesus has since shown his supernatural, miraculous power by restoring much of my vision in the damaged eye, in spite of the doctors telling me that I would never have use of it again!

This eternal Jesus lives and dwells in us. He knows everything about us, just as he knows everything about the Father. All of us are concerned about our hair. We wash it, comb it, set it, braid it, color it, and are disturbed when it turns gray, and even more upset when we lose it. As concerned as we are about our hair, there is one thing we don't know. We don't know how many hairs are on our head. But the One who lives in us knows, for according to Matthew 10:30-31: *And the very hairs of your head are all numbered. So don't be afraid; you are more valuable to him (the Father) than a whole flock of sparrows!*

Jesus says something similar in Matthew 6:30-34. He tells us that our heavenly Father knows all our needs, and as a good Father, he will supply them. Jesus claims that he and the Father are one. Now that Jesus dwells and lives in us, all our needs are known to him! Surely if he loves us enough to live in us, we do not need to be afraid of anything, for he knows exactly what is going to happen. He is never afraid, for he sees everything at all times, and he is in control of all things.

In Psalm 139:1-6, we find that Jesus knows us so well that he knows when we sit down and when we stand up and what we will say, even before we say it. He is not outside of us, looking down on us. Christ is in us! His Spirit, the One who searches the mind of God, now dwells in us and will reveal all truth to us (1 Corinthians 2:11-13).

Since God sees everything and there are no surprises, Jesus can assure us that he will make us to be more than conquerors according to Romans 8:37-39. To be more than conquerors means that nothing in all our life will be so great a surprise as to be able to separate us from the love of God. To be more than conquerors means that the final score will be 100 to 0!

What difference does it make to you to understand who and where Jesus is? Jesus is outside, and he is also in heaven at the right hand of the Father, and he is like a light shining down on us. All that is true, but it misses the most wonderful truth of all. Jesus, through his Holy Spirit, dwells in us! His life is in us. We are bonded to him for all eternity. To all who believe, to all who trust him, Jesus has promised to come into them and eat with them (Revelation 3:20)! He pours his life into us, making us new creations, so we never have to fear, because Jesus is never surprised or caught unaware! He is timeless. He is eternal God. He sees everything, and he assures us that he is in total control.

Reflect

1. What have been some of your greatest surprises?

2. Why is Jesus, who is God and thus eternal, never surprised by anything?

3. How much does God know about us (Psalm 139:1-6)?

4. What does God know about our future (Romans 8:37-39)?

5. What difference should it make in our self-image that Jesus, who is the eternal God, dwells in us?

who do you look like?

Prayer

Dear Jesus, I cannot understand all of this. You are so much more than merely a good teacher or a great man of God. You are God in human flesh. You are in the Father, and the Father is in you. Yet, you are in me. I guess I don't need to understand; I only need to believe and rejoice that I am your dwelling place, your mansion, your temple. Lift my spirits, Jesus, and let me rejoice today. For your sake, I pray. Amen.

Chapter Eleven

Jesus, the Person Who Created Everything... Lives in Us!

He created everything there is. Nothing exists that he didn't make. John 1:3

Each of us has enough blood vessels in our body that, if stretched out, they would circle the globe. We have over 25,000 miles of veins, arteries, and capillaries. These blood vessels are like highways, traveled every few seconds by 25 to 30 trillion red blood cells. Each of these blood cells lives for about 120 days. To replace those that wear out, the bone marrow must produce about 200 billion new red cells daily, or 2 to 3 million every second, 24 hours a day! These cells are like little trucks, and our lungs

who do you look like?

are the loading docks. Passing through the heart, these little red trucks pause in the lungs, where they are loaded with oxygen, and when the heart beats, they are sent throughout the body to deliver that oxygen to every cell. When they unload it, each red blood cell picks up garbage (carbon dioxide) from the cell, and as the heart beats again, they race to the kidneys, where the waste from the cell is unloaded.

In addition to this amazing network of red cells, the Creator put in white cells which are like police cars roaming through our bodies looking for enemy attacks in the form of disease. When they find disease or a wound, they send out a call, and these white cells fly into the area and attack the foreign intruders!

Not only do we not realize what is happening right within our own bodies, but we also cannot understand what is happening in the universe. All of this came into existence, according to Genesis 1:3, because God spoke. God commanded everything that is, to be. John tells us that it was through Jesus, the Word of God, that all things were made. It

JESUS, THE PERSON WHO CREATED EVERYTHING...

was Jesus who designed our bodies, including our red and white blood cells and the amazing system of blood vessels. It is through Jesus that the sun, moon, and stars were put in place.

Quiet streams lined with trees demonstrate our Lord's love of beauty. What kinds of life are in the stream? How many fish make their home there? The endless scenes of nature reveal the greatness of our God. Massive trees grow from tiny shriveled seeds which appear to lack life. Birds flit from tree to tree, each singing a distinctive song of praise. This is the Creator God who has chosen to live and dwell in us! This is a most amazing truth. No wonder it is repeated over and over in the New Testament. Christ in you, the hope of glory (Colossians 1:27). Christ lives in me (Galatians 2:20)! Who is Christ? How important is he? The answer is that he is the One who made all things! He dwells in us through his Holy Spirit.

How can this be? Perhaps part of the answer is found in Genesis 1:26-27, the story of the creation of Adam. God determined that humans would be created in *our image and our likeness*. While we are

who do you look like?

NOT God, we are his closest relatives. He created us to be superior even to the angels, for they are God's servants, his messengers, while we are God's children. God adopts us as his children and heirs. Perhaps this is why Christ, through his Holy Spirit, can dwell in us. We were made to be God's children. We were made to have a living relationship with him. We were made to be branches on the vine of Christ, so that his life might flow through us.

What does having the Creator of the universe live in you do for your sense of value? How does the fact that the Creator of all things, the One through whom all things were made, now dwells in you make you feel about yourself?

Reflect
1. What happened when God spoke (Genesis 1:3), and how does this show the amazing power of God?

2. What is special about the way God created humans, according to Genesis 1:26, 27? What does being created this way mean for

your self-worth? For your self-image? For your self-purpose?

3. What characteristic of all of God's creation is found in Genesis 1:31, and what does this mean?

4. What does having the Creator of everything living in you do for your self-worth?

Prayer

> *Savior, these concepts are so staggering, so awesome that we cannot even start to understand them. How can we, who do not even know the mysteries and miracles of our own bodies, nor understand the stars and planets, begin to appreciate your glory and power and majesty? With tears of joy we bow before you, Lord. How can it be that you should so honor us that you stand before our door daily, knocking and asking if you*

who do you look like?

may come in? How can it be that we are so busy with such trivial concerns that often we do not hear your knock, and in our haste, fail to include you in our lives that day? Forgive us. Cleanse us. And grant us the overwhelming experience of your presence today. For your sake, we pray, Jesus. Amen.

Chapter Twelve

Jesus, the Source of All Life, Lives in Us!

Life itself was in him, and this life gives light to everyone. John 1:4

Nothing is more important to us than life. We are consumed with living. We eat to live. We work to provide food to eat so that we can nourish life. We sleep to live. When we get sick, we are concerned about possibly dying. Health magazines abound. Dozens of new diets are peddled every week. Hundreds of millions of dollars are spent on prescription drugs every week of the year! We all are searching for that eternal fountain of life. Where can we find that power we need to live forever?

Christ, according to John 1:4, is the author of all

life. Think of that right now—the author of eternal life lives in all who believe in him. Jesus claimed the title of author of life, for himself when, standing before a distraught sister whose brother Lazarus had died, he said, *I am the resurrection and the life. Those who believe in me, even though they die like everyone else, will live again. They are given eternal life for believing in me and will never perish. Do you believe this, Martha?* (John 11:25-26)? Can you imagine a mere man making a claim like that? Think about these words: ...*whoever believes in me, even though they die, will live again.* If you think that Jesus is not God, but only a good man with high morality, you are not being rational. The author, C.S. Lewis, said that if Jesus were not really God, it would be easier to believe in him if he claimed to be a poached egg! We only have two choices about Jesus. Either he is what he claimed to be, namely the author and source of all forms of life, or he was the greatest hoax ever perpetrated.

While scientists understand many things, the mystery of life still escapes them. We can paint a picture of a flower, and we can build a model flower, but we cannot create a real flower. No one fully understands the mystery of life contained in a seed. A little seed, so hard, planted in moist earth and bathed with sunlight, bursts into a new plant that in time produces a glorious flower. One kernel of corn, planted in the ground, can produce a stalk bearing a minimum of six hundred kernels! The springtime fields and mountainsides are graced with flowers: reds and yellows, blues and purples. All over planet earth, our Savior fills the landscape with a multitude of varieties of life in the form of flowers, birds, fish, animals, and his image-bearers—you and me.

He assures us, that since he lives in us through faith, whoever believes in him will never die. Think about Galatians 2:20 again, *I have been crucified with Christ: and I myself no longer live, but Christ lives in me. And the real life I now have within this body is a result of my trusting in the Son of God who loved me and gave himself for me*. That means that we have eternal life planted in us, beginning the moment we believe in Christ. That life will not die, for Christ is the author of that life. He tells us that as we remain in him and he remains in us, we, as the branches receiving his life, will bear much fruit.

Jesus is the ultimate life giver. He not only gives physical life when a baby is created, but he also gives eternal life. The Bible describes this eternal life as life that comes from imperishable seed and is living and enduring. *For you have been born again, not of perishable seed, but of imperishable, through the living and enduring word of God* (1 Peter 1:23) (NIV). Since the giver of eternal life, Jesus, dwells in us, we become channels through which that eternal life flows to others. Can you conceive of yourself in that way—as a believer in Jesus, do you realize that you are a channel of eternal life? What does that realization do to create purpose in your life? You were born to do good, and the greatest good is spreading eternal life! *For we are God's masterpiece. He has created us anew in Christ Jesus, so that we can do the good things He planned for us long ago* (Ephesians 2:10).

Once Jesus was celebrating a great feast in the temple. The priests were re-enacting an Old Testament vision in which the prophet Ezekiel saw a river of water flowing down from the Temple into the

JESUS, THE SOURCE OF ALL LIFE

Dead Sea, transforming and filling it and its river banks with life (Ezekiel 47). The Jews were dancing and shouting as the priests poured water from their golden pitchers onto the temple floor. Jesus was sitting there watching. Suddenly he stood up and shouted so that everyone could hear him. *On the last day, the climax of the festival, Jesus stood and shouted to the crowds, 'If you are thirsty, come to me! If you believe in me, come and drink! For the Scriptures declare that rivers of living water will flow out from within. (When he said, 'living water' he was speaking of the Spirit, who would be given to everyone believing in him. But the Spirit had not yet been given, because Jesus had not yet entered into this glory). Jesus stood and said in a loud voice, "If anyone is thirsty, let him come to me and drink.* (John 7:37-39). While this translation says rivers of living water, the literal translation is torrents of living water. Living water is that which gives eternal life. Can you imagine that because Jesus is in you, torrents of eternal life can flow from you? What does that do for your image of yourself? Can there be anything more important to this world than people who have the fountain of life in them? By planting the

who do you look like?

imperishable seed of living and enduring life (the Bible), we can see eternal, transforming life spring up in others.

Praise the Savior. Bow humbly before this awesome God, knowing that he loves you so much that he has made you his dwelling place. When you think of the fact that Christ lives in you, remember who it is that should now occupy the central place in your heart. Think about what you have learned about the One who lives in you.

- He is the One who reveals God and relates us to our Father.
- He is the only Way to the Father, the true God, and he lives in us!
- He is the One who shows us the greatness of God, but far more than this, he shows us the love of God by his sacrifice for our sins. This Jesus lives in us!
- He is the One who is the beginning and the end of everything. He is timeless, and he is eternal. There are no surprises for our Savior. He knows everything that can be known. And he lives in us!

- He is the Creator of all things and he is the One who made us in his image. And he lives in us!
- He is the Source of all life and this Source of all life lives in us, assuring us that if we trust him, we will never die. Praise his name forever!

Reflect

1. Who is the Creator of all life?
2. How does Jesus describe himself in John 11:25, and what do you think that means?
3. How close are we to the Creator of life, according to John 15:1-5?
4. List the five descriptions of Christ presented in this lesson, according to John 1:1-4. Explain what difference it makes to know that this person is knocking at your door daily, asking to be included in your life.

Prayer

Precious Savior, you are the source of all life. You know how concerned I am about my body. Help me to understand that through trusting you, my heart has been opened to your presence. Help me to see that I am more than this body—that I am spirit, soul and body, and that I will continue to exist apart from my body when I die. Help me trust that when you return, my body will be resurrected as a glorious, spiritual and eternal body, free from all sickness and death. I give you thanks and praise that you live in me and are the source of all life. In your name, I pray. Amen.

PART THREE

Acceptance

One of the most amazing characteristics of Jesus is his ability to accept us and forgive us for all the wrongs we have done. He did this by bearing our punishment. He paid our spiritual debt in full. His forgiveness is not some cheap, sentimental, meaningless forgiveness. When Jesus forgives and accepts us, it means that all wrong has been made right! When Jesus comes into us, he makes it just as if we never sinned. He shines out of us when we, responding to the fullness of complete forgiveness, knowing that our debts have been canceled and that we have been accepted back, no longer insist on our rights or nourish the spiritual cancers of jealousy, revenge and hatred. In our own emptiness, we cannot forgive. When Christ fills us, however, we can from that fullness, forgive others, for our fullness does not come from gaining revenge but rather comes from Christ's indwelling

who do you look like?

Spirit. Forgiveness is one of Christ's most attractive features, and when it graces us, we become beautiful to all.

> *Because one person disobeyed God,*
> *many people became sinners. But because*
> *one other person (Christ) obeyed God, many people*
> *will be made right in God's sight.*
> Romans 5:19

> *And forgive us our sins, just as we have forgiven*
> *those who sin against us.* Matthew 6:12

> Float this verse during Part Three
> *And while he was still a long distance away,*
> *his father saw him coming. Filled with love and*
> *compassion, he ran to his son, embraced him and*
> *kissed him.* (Luke 15:20)

Chapter Thirteen

Christ's Acceptance of Others

*And Jesus said,
"Father, forgive these people, because they don't know what they are doing."*
Luke 23:34

We have seen the importance of the One who lives in us. He is the only way to know God and to be loved by our Father. He reveals who God is, and he relates us to God. He shows us God's greatness, not merely in creation but even more by demonstrating God's ability to stoop down to love us. He is never surprised, because he is eternal, and he is omniscient (all-knowing). He is the creator of all that exists, and he is the source of all life.

In the remaining four parts we are going to examine what Jesus looks like. What impressions

who do you look like?

did he make on people when he walked on this earth? What attracted crowds of thousands to him? What kind of people did Jesus attract? Were they the poor, the cast-offs, the criminals, and the refugees of society? Or were they the wealthy and the religious leaders of his day? Many are surprised to find out that most of the people who were attracted to Jesus were poor, ordinary, common folks. It was the well-known, religious leaders of his day, who hated him and finally arranged for his crucifixion. He was accepting of the least of the people, and he brought them dignity. It was obvious that he was the kind of friend everyone wanted. Through his acceptance of all people, even the worst, and through the dignity he gave them and the friendship he offered them, he brought about in them a whole new purpose for living!

If so great a being lives in us and shines out of us, this means that we, too, will, at least in some ways, display Jesus' characteristic of acceptance of others, and we will bring dignity to them. We, too, will attract friends, and in so doing, we will find a whole new purpose in life! Jesus told us we would do greater works than he did! *The truth is, anyone who believes in me will do the same works I have done, and even greater works, because I am going to be with the Father* (John 14:12).

Jesus is in us, spiritually. Christ is also with the Father in heaven. He is present everywhere, since he is God. He is especially present in us, through his Holy Spirit. Since his Spirit is in us, his power also dwells in us.

One of the greatest demonstrations of Christ's supernatural power in accepting others occurred as he was nailed to the cross. It was the power to forgive. As the nails were being driven into his hands and feet, and the cross was raised in place, he prayed that his Father would forgive those who were doing this horrible thing. That same forgiving, accepting power is now flowing through us, because he lives in us. Family fights should be stopping as we accept one another in forgiveness. Quarreling should be ceasing. In place of hatred, there should be love. In place of selfishness, there should be selfless sacrifice. In place of blindness to others' needs, there should be tender and compas-

who do you look like?

sionate sight. While Christ demonstrated this in his life in Palestine for the thirty-three years he lived on earth, it is now being demonstrated worldwide through the lives of his believers. Far greater works of acceptance are being demonstrated all over the world than those that Jesus alone performed while he walked on earth! Christ's acceptance of sinners radiates in some form from every believer. This is what Jesus meant when he said that we who believe would do greater works than those he did. He set the model of perfect acceptance and then, upon his resurrection and ascension, moved, through the outpouring of his Holy Spirit, into the heart of every believer.

There was a terrible persecution of Christians in the state of Orissa, India early in the 21st century. Tens of thousands of Christians were driven from their homes. This number included a pastor, his wife and their children. They fled from their home into the jungle only to watch, from hiding, their persecutors beat, rape and kill their fellow Christians. This outpouring of hatred was reported throughout India and the world, and the perpetrators were

CHRIST'S ACCEPTANCE OF OTHERS

forced to stop. A few days later the pastor and his wife and children returned home and began ministering, not just to the few Christians who were left, but also to the Hindu and Muslim neighbors who had persecuted them. In the months that followed, this pastor reported that he had baptized more people in three months than he had in the previous seven years combined! Those who had so recently been persecutors, stated that they were mystified by and drawn to the pastor's gentle spirit of acceptance of those who had committed such horrible crimes. They could not understand how he could love people who had done the things they had done. That pastor looked like Jesus, the epitome of forgiveness and acceptance. This should be the goal of every believer, namely, to live in the power and fullness of the Savior who forgave even those who nailed him to the cross. To resemble Jesus means that people see us as those who have supernatural power to accept and forgive even the worst of those who have wronged us.

Jesus told a story about a cruel son who insulted his father and ran away with his inheritance, squandering it all. He became so poor that he had no money and wound up eating the food of the pigs he was attending! He decided to return home. His father was waiting for him, looking down the road. When he saw him far, far down the road he ran to embrace him! We will study the father's forgiveness of this boy, for it is a picture of Jesus' forgiveness of us. We will examine five aspects of Jesus' acceptance and forgiveness of others, five aspects of the forgiveness and acceptance that shine in Jesus. These are five characteristics of acceptance that should shine from us if Christ lives in us.

1. <u>The immediate acceptance</u> and forgiveness of others.
2. <u>The eagerness</u> to accept and forgive others.
3. <u>The amazing results</u> of being forgiven and accepted by God.
4. <u>The reason</u> we can be accepted and can accept others.
5. <u>The unique power</u> of Christ, enabling us to accept others.

Reflect

1. In your own words, write out the five characteristics of acceptance.
2. What amazing promise did Jesus give us in John 14:12?
3. How does John 15:5 explain why we can show Christ's amazing acceptance and forgiveness of others?

Prayer

Precious Savior, help me to see, feel, and enjoy your supernatural power to forgive me. For your sake I pray, Jesus. Amen.

Chapter Fourteen

Jesus' Immediate Acceptance of Sinners

The Parable of the Lost Son
Luke 15:11-32
New Living Translation (NLT)

¹¹ ... Jesus told them this story: "A man had two sons. ¹² The younger son told his father, 'I want my share of your estate now instead of waiting until you die.' So his father agreed to divide his wealth between his sons. ¹³ A few days later this younger son packed all his belongings and moved to a distant land, and there he wasted all his money in wild living. ¹⁴ About the time his money ran out, a great famine swept over the land, and he began to starve. ¹⁵ He persuaded a local farmer to hire him, and the man sent him into his fields to feed the pigs.

¹⁶ "The young man became so hungry that even the pods he was feeding the pigs looked good to him. But no one gave him anything. ¹⁷ When he finally came to his senses, he said to himself, 'At home even the hired servants have food enough to spare, and here I am dying of hunger! ¹⁸ I will go home to my father and say, Father, I have sinned against both heaven

JESUS' IMMEDIATE ACCEPTANCE OF SINNERS

and you, [19] and I am no longer worthy of being called your son. Please take me on as a hired servant.'"

[20] *"So he returned home to his father. And while he was still a long way off, his father saw him coming. Filled with love and compassion, he ran to his son, embraced him, and kissed him. [21] His son said to him, 'Father, I have sinned against both heaven and you, and I am no longer worthy of being called your son.'[22] "But his father said to the servants, 'Quick! Bring the finest robe in the house and put it on him. Get a ring for his finger and sandals for his feet. [23] And kill the calf we have been fattening. We must celebrate with a feast, [24] for this son of mine was dead and has now returned to life. He was lost, but now he is found.' So the party began.*

[25] *"Meanwhile, the older son was in the fields working. When he returned home, he heard music and dancing in the house, [26] and he asked one of the servants what was going on.[27] 'Your brother is back,' he was told, 'and your father has killed the fattened calf. We are celebrating because of his safe return.'[28] The older brother was angry and wouldn't go in. His father came out and begged him,[29] but he replied, 'All these years I've slaved for you and never once refused to do a single thing you told me to. And in all that time you never gave me even one young goat for a feast with my friends. [30] Yet when this son of yours comes back after squandering your money on prostitutes, you celebrate by killing the fattened calf!' [31] His father said to him, 'Look, dear son, you have always stayed by me, and everything I have is yours. [32] We*

who do you look like?

had to celebrate this happy day. For your brother was dead and has come back to life! He was lost, but now he is found!"'

And while he was still a long way off...
Luke 15:20

This story, recorded in Luke 15, is a very unusual one. Part of the story was very well known. It was a favorite story which the rabbis of Jesus' day told frequently, but with a radically different ending than the one Jesus gave to it. In the rabbis' version, the father refused to accept his wayward son and forgive him. The son was permanently excommunicated from the family. Jesus gave the story an amazing new ending, saying that the father was waiting on the road for his wayward son to come home. He was so eager to accept this sinful boy back that each day he went out on the road, and with great longing, looked far into the distance to see if his son was returning. Often called the *Parable of the Prodigal Son*, this story is really about the waiting and accepting Father.

As Jesus pictures the father standing on the road day after day, longing and looking for the

JESUS' IMMEDIATE ACCEPTANCE OF SINNERS

return of his son, he is picturing the Father in heaven's eagerness to forgive and accept us back. Since Jesus claimed that he and the Father are one, the Father's eagerness is his eagerness to welcome sinful children. And, since Christ is in us, this must be a picture of what we look like.

The time when the father forgave his son is important. It was when he was still a long way off. It was immediate. We often insist that in order to be forgiven and accepted, a person must first make amends. We want the person to return all the way! We wait until the person proves himself or herself. But God doesn't demand this of us. He has made everything right through the death of Jesus his Son. All he asks for is a basic decision to turn around and begin to walk back to him. He doesn't measure the distance we have to come before he offers us forgiveness. He doesn't say you have to do this, or make those amends. He looks only for us to turn around and start walking back toward him; his forgiveness is immediate.

God accepts us back even if our motives for coming back are mixed up. This son returned home,

who do you look like?

not first of all because he wanted to apologize for hurting his father, but because he was starving and realized that even his father's servants were better off than he was. Yes, he was sorry for what he had done, but it was the misery of his condition that drove him to turn. However, that was overlooked by the father. The father was only concerned that his son had turned toward home. Nothing else mattered, and while he was still a long, long way away, he rushed to him.

There is another illustration of this in the story of a young man who squandered his life in sin and finally wanted to return home but feared his parents would never accept him back. He shared his desire to come home with a friend, and asked that friend to talk to his parents; if they were willing at least to talk to him, he asked his friend to tell them to please tie a white handkerchief on one of the branches of the tree in the front yard. The friend did as he was asked and told the boy that his parents would accept him back, and that he could look for that white handkerchief as a sign of their acceptance of him. He was still very apprehensive.

JESUS' IMMEDIATE ACCEPTANCE OF SINNERS

He took the bus back to the city, and it drove past his house. The boy hardly dared to look out the window, but when he did, he saw not one white handkerchief tied on the tree, but one hundred handkerchiefs covering the tree!

Jesus has a hundred handkerchiefs tied on his tree! He is that eager to accept each of us! This is why he attracted such huge crowds of common, ordinary people. However, even the few powerful people who were secretly lonely and felt that they were failures were warmly accepted by him.

Jesus' power to accept all who feel they need him is a tremendous comfort. We have all sinned. God doesn't wait until we prove ourselves. He, like the father in Jesus' story, is waiting for us, and he sees us while we are yet a long way off. This is the Savior who lives in us! How could we possibly harbor hatred and the desire for revenge and not accept others, while at the same time claim Jesus as our Savior? No, in our own weak, sinful, human power we cannot forgive. But human ability is not Jesus' power. If we surrender to Jesus and ask him to do through us things we cannot even imagine,

who do you look like?

we will release his forgiving power in us. We will stand with that father in the story, looking down the road with eagerness, waiting for the moment of reconciliation with father or mother or brother or sister or business partner or friend, or estranged spouse, longing for that moment of making it right between us. Are you ready, in Christ's power, to look like Jesus and hang a hundred white handkerchiefs of acceptance on your tree in your front yard?

Reflect

1. According to Luke 15:20, what did the son do to begin the process of forgiveness?

2. When did the father respond and offer forgiveness? Was it after the boy returned all the way home, or just as he started to return? What does this tell us about our Father in heaven?

3. What were the boy's motives in returning home? Were they a selfish concern for himself or a selfless concern for the father? What does this tell us about God's willingness to forgive us?

Prayer

Dear Savior, it is hard to understand that you are just waiting for me to turn around, to come toward you. It seems to me that I should have to do more than merely trust you. Somehow, Lord, I feel I need to win your approval, and yet you tell me that you are waiting and watching for my return. Come now, Lord Jesus, into my heart. Please. I need your supernatural power. In your name, I pray. Amen.

Chapter Fifteen

Jesus' Eagerness to Forgive

But while he was still a long distance away, his father saw him coming. Filled with love and compassion, he ran to his son, embraced him and kissed him. Luke 15:20

The father's eagerness to forgive was so great that it forced him to run toward this son who sinned against him. The picture of the running father is very unique because fathers in Jesus' time did not run. It was undignified. They especially did not run to greet someone who had sinned against them as badly as this son had sinned. He had shown no consideration for his father's feelings. He dishonored the family name. He demanded his inheritance before his father died and thus displayed his hard-hearted selfishness. It is unlikely that any human father would have been willing to forgive such a sinful son, much less run to greet him as he started to return.

All of us are reluctant to forgive. It is hard to forgive and accept. We nurture our hurt feelings. We enjoy thoughts of revenge. We delight in making our enemies crawl. We refuse to speak to those who once were closest to us because of the pain that they inflicted on us. We want to protect ourselves from being hurt again by never accepting them back.

Nurturing hatred is like nurturing a spiritual cancer. The resulting bitterness will spread and kill. Christ came to set us free from the bondage of hate and revenge. That freedom begins by recognizing the power of the heavenly Father to forgive us, as illustrated in this story. Forgiveness starts while the boy is a long way away, and expresses itself in the eager, but rather undignified, running of the father toward him. The father doesn't wait to find out the boy's motives or to see if the repentance is genuine. He is so eager for forgiveness and acceptance that he races to embrace his long-lost son.

who do you look like?

Since Christ is in us, this is the kind of power for forgiveness and acceptance of others that is flowing through us. As we rejoice in God's eagerness to forgive us, we can also rejoice in our new eagerness to let that forgiveness flow through us to those who have hurt us. True forgiveness from God always overflows in forgiveness of others.

Picture it this way. When Jesus taught us his model prayer, one of the petitions goes like this: ... *And forgive us our sins, just as we have forgiven those who have sinned against us.* (Matthew 6:12). Other translations use the word debt and render it *forgive us our debts.* Think about debt. Most of us are in debt. Think of someone saying to you, *Everything you owe is canceled! You are set free!* What would you feel like? What burden would such freedom remove? That's what God's forgiveness is—it is the cancellation of the spiritual debt that we rack up every day, a debt far larger than any of us realizes. It is Jesus' eagerness to accept us back, even while we are a long way off! God is thrilled at his ability to forgive us, so thrilled that he wants us to share in that joy by forgiving and accepting others. That is why Jesus added *as we forgive our debtors* to the prayer he taught us to pray. It is to encourage us to forgive those who have robbed us spiritually. He assures us that there is no greater joy than to be free of both the debt we owe to God and free of the debt others owe to us. When we reach this level of forgiveness, we know that we are looking like Jesus, the person who lives in us.

God's power to forgive us is the same power that enables us to forgive others! What we cannot do, God can do. We are Christ's body, and we are to release his accepting power in us to enable us to be accepting of others. Christ's power is shown in our eagerness to forgive and in our anticipation of the joy we will feel at being reconciled to each other.

Reflect

1. Why do we need Christ's supernatural, mysterious, inexplicable power to forgive others?

2. God is eager to forgive us. Why do we find this hard to believe?

who do you look like?

3. God is so eager to forgive us that he does not wait for us to come all the way back to Him, but runs to us while we are still a long way off. Is there someone you need to forgive? How can we "run" towards these people, who have hurt us, while still a long way off?

Prayer

> *Precious Savior, help me to trust that you have forgiven me. Help me to see that you are able to forgive me since you have paid my debt. Help me to understand that you cover me with your perfection so that I can stand before the Father clothed in what you have done, and not in my failures. And in that feeling of being set free help me to accept and free those who have sinned against me. I pray this in your name and power, Jesus. Amen.*

Chapter Sixteen

Jesus' Acceptance Brings Amazing Results!

…Quick! Bring the finest robe in the house and put it on him. Get a ring for his finger and sandals for his feet. Luke 15: 22

Nice clothes make us feel good; they improve our self-image. Perhaps no other nation on earth provides such elegant clothing for women as does India. Brides are clothed in the richest garments parents can buy, and adorned with gold jewelry. Grooms are dressed in the finest white clothes and ride to their bride on a white stallion. Weddings in India are extremely expensive. They are the great parties of a lifetime. It is the same in the West. The bride and her mother and friends spend months in finding just the right dresses for the bride and for the ladies in the wedding party.

who do you look like?

Nothing does so much for one's self-image and sense of value, however, as the robes that God puts on us after he has accepted us. One of the most beautiful descriptions of these robes is found in Isaiah 61:10: *I am overwhelmed with joy in the Lord my God! For he has dressed me with the clothing of salvation and draped me in a robe of righteousness. I am like a bridegroom in his wedding suit or a bride with her jewels.*

As we picture Christ living in us, we should be delighted. People who get dressed up for a wedding are excited. This is their finest moment. Isaiah tells us that God has dressed us up in wedding clothes! Because we are clothed in Christ's righteousness, we can be accepted. In our Father's sight, sin no longer soils us. He has placed the robes of righteousness on us. These are white robes (Revelation 6:11). Our spirits should soar as we try to imagine how beautiful we will look to our Father, dressed in the perfect robes of his only Son. In Isaiah 62, God describes his people as being his precious maiden, his bride. All who believe are the bride of Jesus. We will wear a crown of splendor on our heads. Isaiah

JESUS' ACCEPTANCE BRINGS AMAZING RESULTS!

says, *Then God will rejoice over you as a bridegroom rejoices over his bride* (Isaiah 62:5)! Jesus says that when he comes again, he will throw a great wedding feast and we will be joined to him in love for all eternity. This is the Jesus who lives in us—he has cleansed us and accepted us. He has paid our debt. He has washed us and clothed us in the white robes of his perfection. Look inside! See who really is there, through your belief in him!

Acceptance by Jesus doesn't merely result in receiving new, spiritual clothing. God gives us a ring, the family ring. In Jesus' day, the ring was a symbol of authority, just as it still is in monarchies. The king's seal or ring, stamped on documents, made them official. When Christ becomes our representative, covering us with his perfect obedience and his eternal death for our sins, then the Father immediately restores us to a position of great authority. This is described in Matthew 18:18: *I tell you the truth, whatever you bind on earth will be bound in heaven, and whatever you loose on earth will be loosed in heaven (NIV)*. Because Christ is in us, his authority is in us. We can, in the name of Jesus who lives in us, bind evil spirits. Since Christ is in us and we are in him, having taken him as our new head and representative, we now share in his authority. Jesus has defeated all the demonic spirits, and that Jesus lives in us when we believe in him! We must not walk around and act as if we are defeated! The evil spirits are the defeated ones, not we!

A beautiful summary of this is found in Colossians 2:13-15. *You were dead because of your sins and because your sinful nature was not yet cut away. Then God made you alive with Christ. He forgave all our sins. He canceled the record that contained the charges against us. He took it and destroyed it by nailing it to Christ's cross. In this way, God disarmed the evil rulers and authorities. He shamed them publically by his victory over them on the cross of Christ.*

Finally, the father puts sandals on the son's feet. This is a symbol that the wayward son has been restored to full status in the family. The father has accepted him back, and now he is his true child again. This is what God does for us through the power of forgiveness. *Behold, what manner of love the Father has lavished on us that we should be called children of God and such we are* (I John 3:1 NIV).

JESUS' ACCEPTANCE BRINGS AMAZING RESULTS!

Think of what Jesus' forgiveness involves! He is waiting so eagerly for us to turn in faith to him that he pictures himself as running to us. Jesus has paid the ultimate price by his death on the cross so that we might be acceptable to God! God the Father gave Jesus his Son to pay our sin debt, even while we were still his enemies! After paying such a price, it is understandable that he would rejoice with a grand party for everyone who has accepted his forgiveness. If you believe now and have trusted Jesus as your Savior, there is great joy in heaven among the angels, for another child of God has come home. There is no greater display of power in the whole universe than the power God showed in making his only begotten Son our second representative. He clothes us with the greatest garments in the world, the robes of righteousness. He puts the ring of his authority on our fingers, and he puts sandals on our feet as a further sign of his lavish love in adopting us as his children.

This is the basis of a total transformation. The One who has done all this, Jesus Christ, lives and dwells in us through his Holy Spirit! We are accepted, and

who do you look like?

that acceptance radiates from us and shines on everyone we meet and we begin to look like Jesus.

Reflect

1. Explain what happens when Christ forgives us for our sins.
   - What does the robe stand for (Isaiah 61:10)?
   - What does the ring represent (Matthew 18:18)?
   - What do the sandals represent (I John 3:1)?
2. How far does God remove our sins when he forgives us (Psalm 103:12)? What do you think this means?
3. How does Isaiah 1:18 picture God's power to forgive? What does this mean for you?
4. Why should the feeling expressed in Romans 5:1-2 be the feeling we have when we are forgiven?

PLEASE READ THIS FIRST

Prayer

Thank you, Jesus, for taking my sins away, for making me a part of your family, and for giving me your ring. Fill me with your presence. For your sake, Jesus, I pray. Amen.

who do you look like?

Chapter Seventeen

The Reason Jesus Can Accept Us.

For just as through the disobedience of the one man [Adam—our first representative] the many were made sinners, so also through the obedience of the one man [Jesus—our second representative] the many will be made righteous. Romans 5:19 (NIV)

There is something very unsettling about the story of the father that we have just studied. It just doesn't seem right. The son brought such dishonor to the family and hurt the father so much. Shouldn't something be done to make things right? How can this father ignore all the wrong that has been done, run to greet this son, and throw his arms around this filthy boy? How can he throw a welcome home

THE REASON JESUS CAN ACCEPT US.

party, clothing him with the finest robe in the house, give him the family ring, and put the family shoes on him? Where is the justice? Isn't this merely sloppy sentimentalism? On what basis can God forgive all the horrible wrongs in the world?

Remember that Jesus is telling this story with a double meaning. It is not merely a story about an earthly father. It is a story that reveals the truth about our heavenly Father and his eagerness to forgive us. What Jesus does not explain in the story is why the Father is so eager to forgive us. Why can he forgive us? What is the basis of his accepting us back? What is the reason behind his running to us? How can he accept us?

No other area shows God's love as clearly as his forgiveness. He himself made everything right between us through his Son, Jesus Christ. Paul explains this in Romans 5. He points out that when God created humans, he gave us a representative to act for us. That representative was the first human, Adam. And Adam failed. Adam sinned and plunged the human race into sin. God was not defeated. He provided a second representative to act for us, Jesus Christ, his only Son.

who do you look like?

Through Adam's sin against God (disobedience), death came to everyone, because Adam represented everyone and, he chose to disobey God rather than obeying him. *The sin of this one man, Adam, caused death to rule over us, but all who receive God's wonderful, gracious gift of righteousness will live in triumph over sin and death through this one man Jesus Christ* (Romans 5:17). Jesus was given to us as our second representative. He was not only perfectly obedient (sinless) and thus provided a perfect righteousness for all who choose him as their representative, but he also provided the complete penalty for all our sins when he died on the cross in our place. This was a legal punishment. He was not murdered, but he was executed as a criminal, even though he was innocent and sinless. In that death he fulfilled our punishment. He did not die for himself. He died for us. Thus, God our Father, by providing us with a second representative who gave the perfect obedience that Adam failed to give, and who also paid our eternal punishment for sin with his life, now sets before us the choice of which representative we want to follow.

THE REASON JESUS CAN ACCEPT US.

When we trust Jesus and believe in him, we elect him to be our representative. He acts for us. *For just as through the disobedience of the one man [Adam—our first representative] the many were made sinners, so also through the obedience of the one man [Jesus—our second representative] the many will be made righteous* (Romans 5:19 NIV).

To have Christ in us means that when we, by faith in Jesus, vote to have him represent us, we are totally, completely covered by his perfect obedience and his eternal payment of our sins. The realization that Jesus now represents us, and that we are in him and he is in us, brings about a profound transformation in our sense of value, self-image, and purpose in life! We have been set free! We are accepted once again by God.

God's eagerness to forgive us is easily understood when we grasp the concept that Jesus is our second representative, and that he has cleared the way back to the Father for us through his life and his sacrificial death. Why wouldn't our Father be eager to accept us after allowing his Son to suffer and die on our behalf? Why wouldn't such a Father

who do you look like?

be standing on the road, looking for our return with great eagerness, and running to greet us when he sees us in the distance?

Reflect

1. What is the function of a "representative"? How is Jesus our representative?

2. *I was crucified with Christ and I no longer live but Christ lives in me* (Galatians 2:20). What does this verse mean to you?

3. Why, in the light of the tremendous work of Jesus, is the Father so eager to forgive us?

THE REASON JESUS CAN ACCEPT US.

Prayer

Thank you, Jesus, for representing me. Thank you for being my representative before God so that I can be completely free of all my sins, because by your presence in me, you make me whiter than snow and clothe me in your righteous clothes. I give my life in thanksgiving to you. For your sake, Jesus, I pray. Amen.

Chapter Eighteen

Jesus' Acceptance of Us, Gives Us the Ability to Accept Others.

Forgive us our sins, just as we have forgiven those who have sinned against us.
Matthew 6:12

(Read: Matthew 18:21-35)

Imagine a picture of a young man and his girl friend. The boy has a stony look on his face and has turned away from the girl. And the girl has a pensive, longing look on her face, as if she is longing for their relationship to be restored. This might be a picture of many troubled relationships. Every person on earth experiences broken relationships and the need to offer forgiveness.

JESUS' ACCEPTANCE OF US...

If forgiveness and acceptance is the greatest display of God's love and power, and if Jesus Christ, (the One in whom that power resides) lives in us, then we should be marvelous examples of accepting and forgiving as well. Readiness to accept others, even those who have sinned against us, is what it means to look like Jesus. Satan realizes that the more we show forgiveness to those who have wronged us, the more Jesus Christ is revealed through us. Satan's primary tools to keep us in sin are the tools of revenge, bitterness and hatred. <u>Satan hates a forgiving disciple of Jesus.</u>

Most people do not understand the benefits of being able to forgive and accept those who sin against them. Here are some examples of the benefits of being able to forgive others.

•When we forgive others, we are assured that we are children of God. Jesus told us that peace-makers are especially blessed, for they will be called sons of God (Matthew 5:9). Peace makers are people who offer forgiveness. Having both experienced and understood the forgiveness God has given, they know that they have no choice but to forgive those who have sinned against them.

who do you look like?

- Second, when we forgive those who persecute us, we will have a great reward in heaven. Jesus says that when people persecute us and say all manner of false lies about us, we should be glad, because we will have a great reward in heaven (Matthew 5:11,12). Jesus says that every time someone hurts us, we have a new opportunity to allow his power to flow from within us to forgive that person. How much we have been wronged and hurt does not matter; Christ's power to forgive is infinite. We are to forgive in Christ's power, not in our own.
- Third, forgiving others is one of the most freeing and liberating experiences we can have. When we harbor thoughts of revenge, we are nurturing a kind of spiritual cancer that enslaves us to hatred. Jesus says that hatred is a form of murder (Matthew 5:21-24). It keeps us from true worship. Jesus says that if we have any problem with another person, we must get it solved immediately, before we worship. When we are consumed with hatred and feel we will never be able to forgive, we must remember, by refusing to forgive, we are living as the old person we were! But now Christ lives in us, and he

is the One who has the ultimate power, the power to forgive. The way in which we are set free, when Christ comes into us, is by getting rid of the heavy burden of hatred and revenge. When we forgive those who have sinned against us, we ourselves are liberated!

• Finally, offering forgiveness is the necessary response to receiving forgiveness. In Matthew 18:21-35, Jesus tells the parable of a servant who had a massive debt forgiven, but in return, refused to forgive a very small debt owed to him. Jesus points out that we have no choice but to forgive others, since God has forgiven us for a lifetime of sin. Forgiving others is the result of being transformed, of wearing the robes of righteousness and the ring of God's authority, and calling ourselves children of the King of Forgiveness. We must forgive those who have sinned against us. The point of the story is that no one could possibly have sinned against us as much as we have sinned against God. Having been forgiven so much, surely we must in turn forgive what others have done against us. We are able to do this, because the Power of Forgiveness, our Lord Jesus, dwells in us, and it is in his power that we can forgive others.

Reflect

1. Suggest several reasons why it is hard to forgive each other. *Pride.*

2. How necessary is it to forgive, according to Matthew 6:12?

3. How does Christ's power in us enable us to forgive, according to the story in Matthew 18:21-35? What did the unmerciful servant forget? How does concentration on the presence of Christ in us enable us not to forget this?

Prayer

Precious Savior, pour your power into me now and enable me to forgive (name) for what has happened. Set me free from my hatred and jealousy. For your sake, I pray. Amen.

PART FOUR

Jesus, the Hope of the World

Depression is a lack of hope; the blues occur when you don't have anything to look forward to. Colossians 2:17 (NIV) reads *Christ in you, the hope of glory.* If Jesus is the hope of glory, then we can anticipate that the primary characteristics of our Savior should shine out of us. One of those primary characteristics is hope.

Building your self-image on the fact that Jesus lives in you means that you will live in anticipation of the future, for hope is anticipating, in a positive way, all that is to come. Virtually all the promises in the Bible talk about positive things that are coming. The classic hope is the one from Romans 8:31-32: *What can we say about such wonderful things as these? If God is for us, who can ever be against us? Since God did not spare even his own Son but gave him up for us all, won't God, who gave us Christ, also give us everything else? Because God did the greatest thing he could in giving us Jesus, why in the world would we think that he would deny us the lesser things. And we know that God causes everything to work together for the good*

who do you look like?

of those who love God and are called according to his purpose for them (Romans 8:28).

Seeds are symbols of hope. We plant seeds in the hope that they will sprout, grow and produce food. Farmers are professional hopers. Farmers don't plant seed with a long face, feeling depressed and hopeless. They plant seed with a purpose, with hope, with anticipation of a harvest. Planting seeds is an expression of hope and anticipation. We plant an acorn and hope to get an oak tree. One kernel of corn can produce six hundred kernels. A little seed that is only about a quarter inch can produce a tree fifty feet high! As spiritual farmers we look into the future with hope and anticipation of a great harvest of spiritual fruit.

Here are the words that we will be considering: *Yes I am the vine; you are the branches. Those who remain in me, and I in them, will produce much fruit. For apart from me you can do nothing.* (John 15:5).

Float this verse during Part Four:
Christ in you, the hope of glory. Colossians 1:27

Chapter Nineteen
The Importance of Hope

There are three things that will endure—faith, hope and love—and the greatest of these is love

(1 Corinthians 13:13)

When I was a little boy, I never wanted to go to heaven. Heaven sounded boring, because everything was perfect. I didn't think there would ever be any change, and that sounded terrible. I would never have anything to look forward to. Heaven was *hopeless*, I thought but I was wrong. The Bible tells us that heaven will be full of eternal, living, never-ending, never disappointing hope. It says, *But now three things endure-faith***,** *hope and love...* (1 Corinthians 13:13). Hope, along with faith and love, is eternal; it endures forever. Hope is looking forward to change. Heaven will be eternal exploration of and growth in the beauty of a God, who has no limits. There will be constant, wonderful change; progress in gaining knowledge; and discovery of new dimensions of God's power and majesty. We will always be looking forward to new exciting experiences of discovering more of God's greatness, and never again will any of these discoveries disappoint us. Since heaven is eternal life, and life is always expressed in growth, and growth means hope, there will be living hope in heaven.

Peter describes the hope we will have in heaven in these words: *Praise be to the God and Father of our Lord Jesus Christ! In his great mercy he has given us new birth into a living hope through the resurrection of Jesus Christ from the dead...* (1 Peter 1:3 NIV). I love that description—a living hope means a hope that never, ever will disappoint or fade. We will never be disappointed with anything in heaven. My father, a chemist, said that hope and anticipation filled his life every time he went into the laboratory to conduct a new experiment. He was always anticipating new discoveries. However, he said that the excitement would fade soon after

THE IMPORTANCE OF HOPE

each discovery. The excitement we will feel about the discoveries we will make in heaven will never, ever fade or grow old. We have been born again to a living hope.

The word hope defines little children. They are bundles of hope, always living in excited, joyful anticipation of what is coming. They are excited about birthdays and about passing from one grade to another in school. None of us would ever want our children to remain the same. The thrill of having children is watching them grow through the various stages of life. To be alive is to be growing. Hope keeps us all going. A person is at the bottom when he says, all hope is gone. One of the great challenges for children raised in poverty is to retain their hope. They need to hope that their lives will change for the better. They cannot grow without hope. Hope drives and motivates us to transform our families, our neighborhoods, our villages, our states, and our nations. We hope our businesses will grow, and if we do not have that anticipation, that hope of growth, our businesses will not grow. It is the expectation and hope for growth that drives

who do you look like?

us all. Changing and improving things gives life meaning and purpose. Hope and joy are partners.

We hope when we hold a small acorn and imagine the potential it holds for becoming a massive oak tree. No one can fully understand how an apparently dead, hard seed, when placed in the ground and watered, can sprout a tiny white ribbon of life, reaching up above the ground. Warmed by the sun and watered by the rain, the little sprout arises, turns green, and begins to grow into a mature tree. First it appears as a little seedling and then a little stem with a few branches. Over the next months and years, it will grow into a huge, oak tree. What made that little seed change so much? Life did it. Wherever there is life there will be hope. Death is like giving up all hope.

While we can work hard to bring about transformation, spiritual growth (which is the ultimate gift for which we can hope) can come only through the life of Jesus flowing into us and through us. That life of Jesus, as we see in John 15:5 will flow and expand in us only when He remains in us, and we remain in him. In other words, just as a seed must be put into the ground in order to germinate and grow into a tree,

THE IMPORTANCE OF HOPE

so also we must meet the condition of remaining in Christ and having Christ remain in us in order to have the life of Christ grow in us. The formula for having hope is the same as the formula for growing seed; the life has to be *planted*. When Jesus' life is planted in us through faith in him, hope springs eternal!

Jesus is the ultimate picture of hope. He attracted people, because he brought hope to them. The crowds followed him, anticipating new life in the forms of healing and transformation. They listened to him, because he spoke words of hope. He talked about a kingdom for which they had hoped, even though it came in a form they did not fully understand while he was with them. As Jesus lives in us, we, too, must be pictures of hope. As we encourage the discouraged, lift those who are burdened, and bring hope to the hopeless, we look like Jesus, the One who lives in us.

Jesus is not only outside of us, but more importantly, Jesus is IN us and, since he is life, there is hope. Understanding what it means to have Jesus in us is the foundation of lasting hope.

The most important, most powerful, most beautiful person in the universe has chosen to live and dwell in our lives. If that doesn't give us reason to anticipate, to look forward, to hope, then nothing can. When we look in and see Jesus, we see the picture of the hope which must radiate from us.

Reflect

1. Why does growth always bring change?

2. What happens when we stop hoping for something better?

3. When does change bring joy?

Prayer

Dear Jesus, grant that I may never lose hope by failing to realize that you, the ultimate reason for hope, live in me. May the joy of anticipation color all my life, and may I be a picture of hope to all I meet. May your promise of hope be the hope of my life. Now unto him who can do exceedingly, abundantly above all I could ever ask for or hope for or imagine . . . (Ephesians 3:20). In your name, Jesus, I pray. Amen.

Chapter Twenty
What We Hope for

…God has chosen to make known among the Gentiles the glorious riches of this mystery, which is Christ in you, the hope of glory.
Colossians 1:27 NIV

I am the vine; you are the branches. John 15:5

It took me a long time after becoming a Christian to be able to answer the question, *Where are you Jesus?* I, along with most Christians, thought of Jesus as someone outside of me. I thought, He is in heaven, or at best, walking beside us, or even carrying us. A careful reading of the New Testament, however, indicates that the relationship we have with Jesus is far more intimate. Jesus is inside of us. *I have been crucified with Christ and I no longer live, but Christ lives in me* (Galatians 2:20). Jesus, the most important person in the universe, pictures himself as standing at the door of our hearts, knocking like a common servant. He wants to come in.

Whenever I looked inside myself, all I saw was failure. I became depressed even though I was a Christian. I thought of Jesus as the light shining down on me, but inside me, I found very little that I liked. I constantly fought the fear of failure, and in that, I certainly was not unique. Then that glorious moment occurred when I was challenged with this question, *Where is the light, John? Where is the light* (Psalm 27:1)? I suddenly realized that the light was inside of me. As I thought of Christ, the life and light of the world, I pictured his beauty and perfection *as* something inside of me! Suddenly I had a new attitude toward myself. *There is reason for hope*, I thought! I'm not just a cumbersome, disjointed, non-athletic person. If Christ lives in me, then there is hope. I have something inside of me over which I can rejoice and which gives me great worth! If all I see when I look inside is me, then I am insulting my Savior. I am sinning against him; I am diminishing him. I must build my attitude on what the Bible

who do you look like?

teaches me about Jesus living in me. Who are we when Jesus dwells in us?

We are His branches! Yes, I am the vine; you are the branches (John 15:5).

As we begin each day, we must remind ourselves that since Christ lives in us, he makes us his branches. A branch produces flowers and fruit. A farmer lives in the hope and anticipation that with enough water, pruning, cultivating and sunshine, his vines will produce grapes. We can live in that same kind of hope—that Jesus will produce fruit through us. We can be filled with the excitement and anticipation that comes from trusting that Jesus will do things through us that are beyond our imagination (Ephesians 3:20). The flowers and fruit are the expression of his life, which flows through the vine into the branches. As Jesus lives in us, pouring his life into us, he is the One who will produce the flowers and the fruit in our lives. We are not on our own, running our own lives with a little help from above! When we earnestly want to change, to become better and more beautiful, to sin less and obey more, to overcome selfishness with selflessness, we need to remember that we are the branches and Jesus, the vine, will pour his life into us to produce this fruit. We must remind ourselves that Jesus lives IN US, and that the life we now live is his life. He is the One who can make an acorn grow to be an oak tree, and he is the One who can bring glorious transformation in us, when we remain in him. We must trust him so much that we can actually anticipate transformation and change and thank him for it, even before it occurs.

We are His body! Now all of you together are Christ's body, and each one of you is a separate and necessary part of it (1 Corinthians 12:27).

Jesus tells us that we are his body, and he is our head. That means that while he is a Spirit and no one can see him, he uses us to show others what he is like. A woman we worked with in India told us a story about how she used to bind up lepers' feet with clean bandages. It was a horrible sight, these scarred and wounded feet, and passers-by would often stop, amazed at her willingness even to touch an untouchable beggar, much less to touch the open wounds on their feet. She became to

who do you look like?

them a picture of Jesus for she was bringing hope to the lepers in her care. She was part of the body of Christ and as the poor villagers surrounded her, watching her carefully, they saw Jesus reflected in her hands and in her tender care.

We are his spiritual house (building)! Don't you realize that all of you together are the temple of God and that the Spirit of God lives in you? (1 Corinthians 3:16). *...And now God is building you, as living stones, into his spiritual temple ...* (1 Peter 2:5).

Because Jesus lives in us, he not only makes us his branches and his body, but also his building, or his spiritual dwelling place. Temples are the homes of the gods. Jesus says he does not live in a stone temple or a brick building, but he lives in us, his disciples. Christ doesn't dwell in fancy churches or ancient cathedrals; he dwells in us and makes us his sanctuaries. We are his sacred dwelling places. Because of that, we need to protect our bodies from sin. We must remember that he lives in us, and he is the light of the world and we his house. Remember the picture of the house with which we started? We are glowing because Christ has made us his dwelling place! When you look at that picture, do you see hope? Think of stumbling through the woods at twilight, looking for shelter and coming upon this house. As the light streams from its windows, and as hope streams from your eyes and your heart, will others see Jesus, the author of hope, in you?

Reflect

1. Have you answered Christ's request in Revelation 3:20? *Look! I have been standing at the door and I am constantly knocking. If anyone hears me calling him and opens the door, I will come in and fellowship with him and he with me* (TLB).

2. When Christ lives in us, we become his body, branches and building. Why does Christ use these three images to describe the church?

3. How do those three things change your sense of self-worth and your self-image?

4. In what way does each one affect your purpose in life?

who do you look like?

Prayer

> *We praise you, Savior, that you are in us, and that being in us, you transform us to be your branches, your body, and the building in which you live! Grant that we may be changed by your life flowing into us and through us. May our growth be as great a transformation as that of a seed growing to become a tree. We praise you that your life in us is eternal life. We praise you that we will forever grow and change into your likeness and will reflect your beauty. For your sake, we pray. Amen.*

Chapter Twenty-One:
Living in Hope

Eternal hope, everlasting anticipation, is trusting that we will climb out of the hole and everything will turn out for good, forever. Living hope never disappoints. God tells us that we can anticipate his working in us to produce things beyond anything we can imagine (Ephesians 3:20). This kind of hope is not the result of crossing our fingers or doing some other superstitious thing; it comes when we are continuously aware that Jesus, the author of hope, is living in us. We remain in hope by reminding ourselves that Jesus is in us, making us his branches, his body, and his dwelling place. We remain in Christ when we are filled with praise that Jesus, the One who conquered evil and the grave, now lives in us. Hope is created when we remind ourselves that Jesus will make us more than conquerors, and we live in eager anticipation of that

who do you look like?

fulfillment (Romans 8:37). We live in the hope and joy of knowing that Jesus will avert all evil or turn it to our profit.

In the second week of our study, we pictured ourselves as being in the White House of the President of the United States, or in the home of the Prime Minister. We asked ourselves what would happen to our self-worth, our self-image and our sense of purpose in life if we were able to meet each week with the leader of our nation. That meeting will never occur for most of us. However, something of infinitely more importance does happen each morning when we remind ourselves of the fact that, because Jesus is in us, we have every right to anticipate that he will lead us, guard us, and provide for us during that day.

This chapter is a review of the verses we learned in Chapter Two. The strength of our hope and our anticipation of what will happen each day is in direct proportion to our awareness of how great Jesus is.

In the beginning the Word already existed (John 1:1). Jesus is the most important Being in the universe, because he is the only person who can reveal who God is. He is the Word or Revelation of God. In revealing God to us, Jesus relates us to God. Words relate us to each other. Unless we know what is on each other's mind, we cannot form bonds of love and friendship. Jesus is God the Father's way of speaking to us, so that we can come to know the Father and be adopted as his children. Hope is born in your heart as you remember that Jesus is God's word, God's revelation of himself. No other person or angel is more important than this, and this is the person who lives in us! Every human being longs to know who God is. The answer to that longing dwells within you, and one of the things you anticipate is that people will see and come to Jesus through your words and example.

. . . *He was with God and he was God* (John 1:1). Jesus is God. The Bible reveals the mystery that while there is only one God, God exists as three equal Persons, Father, Son and Holy Spirit. Jesus was given to us as our representative. While remaining God, he is also human. He acted for us by bearing the punishment for our sins. Since we know that,

who do you look like?

and because Jesus is in us, and his punishment covers our sins, we can anticipate his goodness, mercy, and love to attend us every day of our lives. In Jesus, God reveals his highest form of greatness. This is expressed in the ultimate sacrifice Jesus made for us by dying for our sins. As Paul said to the Romans, *He who did not spare his own Son, but gave him up for us all—how will he not also, along with him, graciously give us all things* (Romans 8:32NIV)? That is our ultimate reason for hope!

He was in the beginning with God (John 1:1). Remember that the One who lives in us is eternal. This means that he has lived forever. It means that everything that ever happened and ever will happen is before him right now. He cannot be surprised. We may be surprised at the events of the day, but Jesus, living in us, sees our day perfectly and completely. Since Jesus never began and never will end, and since Jesus cannot be surprised because he knows all things, we can anticipate his promise, namely that he will avert all evil or turn it for good. The One who lives in us is never surprised!

He created everything there is. Nothing exists that

he didn't make. (John 1:2). What an overwhelming thought! We are the branches, the body, the building or dwelling place, of the Creator of the universe! He is so powerful that merely by speaking all things came to be! Surely if he had enough power to create everything, he has the power to change us for the better. Our hope in him, our anticipation of his constant love and mercy, will never disappoint, because he is the Creator! His creative powers flow into us in new life, lifting our spirits in anticipation of his protection and provision. We are transformed into his likeness by glorious growth, and that growth will go on for eternity, for we can never completely know God.

Life itself was in him and this life gives light to everyone. **(**John 1:1-4). He is life and light! He is the author of all life—the life of the acorn that changes into the oak tree. He is the author of life in a grain of rice, which if planted and transplanted, will grow into a stalk of rice, producing hundreds of new grains. He is the light that causes life to grow and change. Where is he? He lives in us, and we are to remain in him by focusing our minds on him. In I

who do you look like?

John 3:2 this mystery is summed up in this way: *Dear friends, now we are children of God, and what we will be has not yet been made known. But we know that when he appears we shall be like him, for we shall see him as he is* (I John 3:2NIV).

Reflect

1. What are the five descriptions of Jesus found in John 1:1-4?

2. What are the *I am* descriptions Jesus gave himself as recorded in:

    a. John 9:5

    b. John 15:1

    c. John 11:25

    d. John 10:7

    e. John 6:35

3. Are these descriptions easy to use when reminding ourselves of who lives in us?

4. Why is reminding ourselves of who Jesus is so important to maintaining hope and anticipation?

Prayer

Grant, dear Savior, that we may never forget who you are. May we grow constantly in the realization of your majesty and your greatness. Overwhelm us with your love. May we marvel that you are the Way to God. May we know today that you will not be surprised by anything in our lives, for you see it all. Lord, change us. Grow us into your image. For your sake, we pray. Amen.

Chapter Twenty-Two:

The Foundation for Hope!

I am the vine; you are the branches. Those who remain in me, and I in them, will produce much fruit. For apart from me you can do nothing. John 15:5

Jesus tells us, *if your stay joined to me and my words remain in you, you may ask any request you like, and it will be granted. My true disciples produce much fruit. This brings great glory to my Father (John 15: 7-8)*. For what are we to be hoping? What are we anticipating? We are hoping for a great harvest of spiritual fruit which is the most significant thing in life.

We hope for significance. We want our lives to have meaning. Christ defines meaning and significance in farming terms; the more fruit we bear the more our life will have meaning. The farmer hopes for a bumper crop. He anticipates it, and when it occurs, he rejoices for his hopes have been fulfilled.

The fruit Christ desires that we produce for him, the fruit for which we hope and which gives us significance and meaning, are spiritual qualities. These are forgiveness, companionship with him and others, love, kindness, gentleness, patience, and passing on eternal life to others. Paul gives us this list of fruit: *But when the Holy Spirit controls our lives, he will produce this kind of fruit in us: love, joy, peace, patience, kindness, goodness, faithfulness, gentleness and self-control* (Galatians 5:22-23). These are eternal investments which bring lasting rewards, starting right now. Jesus tells us, *Don't store up treasures here on earth, where they can be eaten by moths and get rusty, and where thieves break in and steal. Store your treasures in heaven, where they will never become moth-eaten or rusty and where they will be safe from thieves. Wherever your treasure is, there your heart and thoughts will also be* (Matthew 6:19-21). The return on spiritual fruit is eternal, and the investment already

who do you look like?

multiplies incredibly in this life. The value of the spiritual fruit we produce increases eternally; there never is a down-turn on that spiritual investment. Remaining in Christ is to desire the things that Christ desires for us. When our desires match Christ's, then his life flows into us, and we begin to look like him. Looking like Jesus is the great harvest—that for which we hope and long. When we long to be like him, to look like him, to reveal him through our lives, to let his light shine through us, then he remains in us. These are the fruits of which he speaks. Trees bear fruit to give it away. They don't keep the fruit for themselves. Hope means rejoicing, not so much in what we get, but in what we invest and give to others.

Fruit-bearing starts with cleansing from sin. To want what Christ wants is to want to be rid of selfishness. Sin is darkness, but Christ is Light. When Jesus, as the Light of the World (John 9:4) lives in us, his light shines in every room of our house. Imagine that we are like a big house with a separate room for each of our different activities. We have a room in which we sleep, a room in which we eat, a kitchen, and a room in which we sit and talk with

THE FOUNDATION FOR HOPE!

one another. We want the light of Jesus to shine in every room in our house. We don't want Jesus to live in just some parts of our lives. We want Jesus to shine in every part of our lives, so that we can be like the picture of the house with light shining out from everywhere. Thus, we must clean every room of our hearts, so the purity of Christ may fill it.

King David said: *Search me, O God, and know my heart; test me and know my thoughts. Point out anything in me that offends you, and lead me along the path of everlasting life* (Psalm 139:23-24). Our deepest longing when Christ comes into us must be the longing to be made clean. We want him to search every room, every area of our lives. Remember the function of light? Light destroys darkness! When we invite Jesus into every area of our lives, his light will destroy darkness. As that happens, hope springs up and grows.

Light fills us and changes us from having concern for self to having concern for others. The heart of hopelessness is being enslaved to looking at yourself and serving only yourself. Doing this will eventually destroy all hope. Self-centeredness will always drive God and everyone else away. The sin of our first representative, Adam, was to put his desires before everyone else's. God commanded him not to eat of the tree of the knowledge of good and evil. Adam put God's commands second to his desires. Both Adam and Eve were controlled by selfishness, not by love for God. What Adam and Eve wanted to do, they did! Selfish desires controlled them. When Christ comes into us, he fills us to such an extent that we know we do not need anything more! Selfishness dissolves with the coming of his fullness. We start to bubble over with concern for others and with self-forgetfulness, and we anticipate the joy of bringing joy to others. Self-forgetfulness is the only road to lasting joy.

We can struggle all we want with selfishness, but if we fail to remember Jesus is in us, we will never conquer it. Only by remaining in Jesus through focusing our minds on him will his power flow through us to create the desire to help others. Only Jesus can fill us so full that we get to the point of overflowing. We don't need to get any longer once Jesus has filled us. The power of his life in us will transform us. He will enable us gradually to overcome our selfishness.

Not only do we need a new sense of value and a new self-image, but we also need a new purpose for living. That purpose of living is illustrated in Charles Dickens's play, The Christmas Carol. Scrooge was a miserable, stingy old man. All he thought about was himself. All he wanted was to get more money. He did not care how many people he hurt along the way. He was transformed when he discovered the joy of giving, and as the play ends, Scrooge is seen dancing through the village, for he has found a new, satisfying purpose in life—the purpose of fruit-bearing and giving fruit away. A tree doesn't bear fruit in order to keep it. It bears fruit in order to give it away! In sharing his wealth with others, Scrooge found the happiness he always thought he could find but never had achieved through the gaining of all his wealth.

Overcoming concern for ourselves allows the light within us to shine out to others in concern for them. Because we have a new sense of self-worth, and a new self-image based on the beauty and

who do you look like?

power of Christ, we are set free from the demand to constantly get things for ourselves. We are full. Christ is in us. We are transformed to forgive and to give. Because the Savior has filled all of our needs, we are free to see the needs of others. It is only when Christ fills us that we can be set free from feeling empty and worthless, and we can instead live in anticipation of having a meaningful life. Christ's light will shine out of us when we see the needs of others, and we are no longer blinded by our own needs.

Reflect

1. What is the nature of bearing fruit? (Why do trees bear fruit—to keep it or to give it away?)

2. What is the condition for bearing fruit? Explain why?

3. Can we have sin in us and, at the same time, have Jesus in us? How does Psalm 139: 23-24 answer this?

4. What is the motivation for fruit-bearing?

5. What is the power for fruit-bearing?

6. How does Ephesians 2:8-10 (especially verse 10) describe our new purpose in life?

7. What fruit does Christ want us to bear? (Galatians 5:22)

Prayer

> *Precious Savior, may we always remain in you so that we may grow and change into your likeness. Grant that as we grow, you will produce rich spiritual fruit in our lives. In your name, we pray. Amen.*

Chapter Twenty-Three:
Living Hope

I am the vine; you are the branches. Those who remain in me, and I in them, will produce much fruit. For apart from me you can do nothing.
John 15:5

One of the great stories illustrating the way Jesus works is the story of Jesus feeding five thousand families with five little loaves of bread and two fish. This story is found in John 6:5-13. Jesus was in the middle of a great crowd of people estimated to be about five thousand men. This meant that there were probably about twenty thousand people, counting the women and children. Jesus was concerned about feeding all these people, and so he asked his disciples, *Where shall we buy bread for these people to eat* (John 6:5)? Jesus already knew what he was going to do and asked this question only to test the disciples to find out if they would try to solve the problem on their own, or if they would look to him to solve it.

The disciples failed the test. They were hopeless. One of them said, *Eight months' wages would not buy enough bread for each one to have a bite* (John 6:7)! They scouted through the crowd, and all they could find was a little boy who had five loaves of bread and two fish. They brought it to Jesus, not believing that he could do anything with it.

Jesus told the people to sit down. He took the loaves and fish, prayed to his Father, giving thanks for the food, and then distributed the food to the crowd. Everyone took as much as he wanted. After they had eaten, he told his disciples to gather up everything that was left, and the disciples filled twelve large baskets with the pieces of bread and fish that were left.

In this story Jesus illustrates a double truth. The first truth is that apart from him we can do nothing at all. The second truth is that when we look to him and trust him to work through us, amazing things happen that we never dreamed were possible. When we look to Jesus, we have hope. Paul

who do you look like?

described this when he said, *Now unto him who is able to do exceedingly, abundantly, above all we can ask or imagine . . .* (Ephesians 3;20). Do you anticipate that Jesus can do things through you that are greater than anything you can imagine? This text describes how Jesus will work when we remain in him, and he remains in us. Amazing, transforming, inexplicable things, which are beyond our wildest dreams and imaginations, will happen. If, however, we think of Jesus as being outside of us, and that we must work for him in our own power and strength, we will soon find out that we can do nothing.

It is essential that we learn to build our self-image, not on our own power and looks, but instead on the power of the One who lives in us. When we look to him to transform us, we are looking to the One who fed twenty thousand people with five loaves of bread and two fish! When we try to change ourselves, it amounts to nothing at all. Each day Jesus tests us, just as he tested the disciples. He is constantly asking us how we are going to meet the great challenges in our lives. The apostle Paul understood this when he wrote, *For I can do everything with the help of Christ who gives me the strength I need* (Philippians 4:13). Do you believe this?

Reflect

1. What test did Jesus set before his disciples in John 6:7?

2. How did the disciples fail the test? How did they pass the test?

3. How did this miracle illustrate what is said in Ephesians 3:20?

4. What is the danger in living by our *common sense*?

Prayer

Precious Savior, we acknowledge that apart from you remaining in us and our remaining in you, we can do nothing. Thank you for the story of the five loaves and the two fish. Thank you for reminding us that when you worked with that little boy, his lunch was multiplied supernaturally to feed thousands of people! Help us to have that kind of faith. You work with us in unusual ways as we trust your power within us and constantly remind ourselves of who you are. For your sake, Jesus, we pray.
Amen.

Chapter Twenty-Four

Hopelessness

I am the vine; you are the branches.
If a man remains in me and I in him,
he will bear much fruit:
apart from me you can do nothing.
If anyone does not remain in me, he is like a branch
that is thrown away and withers....
John 15:5-6NIV

Jesus gives us a stern warning in this teaching about remaining in him so that he can remain in us. Along with the blessings God promises us, come responsibilities. We have a responsibility to remain in Christ, for if we detach ourselves from the vine, we become a dead branch, and we lose the blessing of his presence in us. A scuba diver who thinks he can get along without relying on his oxygen tanks won't live long under water. Thus, we must

who do you look like?

be serious and disciplined about remaining in him, so that he will remain in us, or we may become like dead branches, and dead branches are without hope of producing fruit. Obviously, any branch cut off from the vine will wither and die. No branch separated from the vine can support leaves or fruit on its own. It must be in the vine to grow. So too, the most important goal of our life must be to have Christ in us. He is like oxygen to the scuba diver, like the vine to the branch. We cannot live without him, for he is our life.

Many of us do not understand this simple truth. We try to build our sense of value apart from Christ's presence in us. We go days without thinking of anything but our own failure or success. We become anxious and worried, or proud and giddy with what we have or have not done. But we seldom rejoice during the day over the fact that we are occupied by Jesus. And this is as senseless as a branch saying to the vine, *I don't need you!* To live apart from Christ is death. It is like a deep sea diver saying that he doesn't need his air tanks any longer. It is like someone saying, *I don't need to eat any longer. I can do just as well without any food.* That person eventually starves to death.

The reason for depression and sadness is the emptiness and the spiritual hunger that we all feel when we refuse to recognize Jesus living in us through his Holy Spirit. We are frustrated because we cannot change ourselves. We feel weak and worthless, and that robs us of vision and courage. We are afraid and anxious about the future. We lack courage and sit around, afraid to attempt anything. All of these are signs of having been cut off from the vine, Jesus Christ, and, instead, depending on ourselves. Dreams evaporate and visions cease. We gradually die without his life flowing into us. To have Jesus in us, and to live his life, will result in excitement, amazement and our constant transformation for good.

To be connected to Jesus is simply to trust him and rely on him rather than relying on our self. Pictures help us to understand. Think of a little child's relationship to loving parents. Jesus used that illustration in Matthew 18:2-3NIV: *He called a little child and had him stand among them. And he said:*

who do you look like?

"I tell you the truth, unless you change and become like little children you will never enter the kingdom of heaven." Christ was referring to the dependency of children upon their parents. Whenever they are in trouble, or hungry, or frightened they rush to Mommy or Daddy. They care nothing about the stock market. They have few anxieties when they have loving parents, for they are totally dependent on their parent's love and care. We must be like little children, snuggling up on their parents' lap and hearing them say, *Everything's OK; Mommy is here.*

The prophet Zephaniah put it so beautifully: *Do not fear O Zion; do not let your hands hang limp. The Lord your God is with you, he is mighty to save. He will take great delight in you, he will quiet you with his love, he will rejoice over you with singing* (Zephaniah 3:16-17) (NIV) If you have trouble understanding what it means to remain in Christ, picture yourself as a little child, sitting on Daddy's lap, without a care in the world, listening to Daddy or Mommy rejoicing over you with singing.

Christ's life, flowing into us, is that which gives us value and hope, dignity and dreams. When we trust him as little children trust their parents, without questioning them, he will work in us in ways that are beyond our imaginations. Christ's life in us is that which illuminates us and radiates from us, giving us beauty that attracts others to him. Christ's life within us ensures that we shall live forever, for the life he gives is eternal life. *For God so loved the world that whoever believes in him should not perish but have eternal life* (John 3:16).

Reflect

1. Why do we all have feelings of worthlessness at times?

2. How important is it to remain in Christ and have Christ remain in us? Give at least the two reasons from the text at the beginning of this meditation, but more if you can.

3. A young Christian businessman was very successful, making over one hundred million dollars in fifteen years. Then he made a bad investment and lost most of his money. Years later, he said that the best years of his life were

who do you look like?

not when he was so materially successful, but instead were when he was a failure in the world's eyes. Can you explain why someone would say this?

Prayer

> *Precious Savior, grant that we may never be cut off from you. Forgive us for living our lives as if you did not exist. May we daily be conscious of your presence. May we always remind ourselves that you are in us, and that you are the greatest Being in the universe. May we always look to you to do that which is beyond our dreams and imaginations. By abiding in you, grant that we may bear rich fruit. In your name we pray, Jesus. Amen.*

PART FIVE

Friendship is praying continuously.

To look like Jesus requires constant contact with him. This is done in many different ways, not only by talking to him, but also by listening to him. It involves taking a thought from the Bible each day and looking at everything that happens that day through spiritual glasses; seeing everything in that day as happening in the light of a special verse. As we discover the new power in listening prayer, our confidence and joy will dramatically increase; and the more we pray, the more we will look like Jesus.

Each section of meditations has been introduced with a float verse. This is different than what you have been doing in taking one verse for all the chapters in a section. Because this section is based on the Lord's Prayer I am assuming that most Christians are very familiar with it. Thus you should have no difficulty in remembering it and using a different phrase each day as spiritual glasses through which you view everything that happens and every decision you must make.

Chapter Twenty-Five

Friendship Is Listening to Each Other

Float this verse today;
Pray without ceasing. (1 Thessalonians 5:17) (NIV)

A pastor was preaching when he suddenly and unexpectedly walked from the pulpit, into the audience, and stopped by Jim. *Hi, Jim,* he said, interrupting his sermon, *How are you feeling today?* Startled, Jim didn't quite know how to respond, so he said, *OK*, but nothing more. The preacher started preaching again, walking further into the audience. He stopped at Frank, asking, *Hey, Frank, do you like the weather today?* Frank, not quite as surprised now as Jim had been, replied, *Yes, it's great, but it could be a little warmer. Well*, the pastor continued, *It is still warmer than expected, and with all that grey weather we've been having, I sure am glad to see the sun shine again.* And with that he started preaching again.

He then walked up into the balcony, interrupting his sermon to talk to someone there. Then he walked out to the nursery to talk to the children there, all the time interrupting himself and then continuing on with his sermon. Finally, he came back up to the pulpit, and by this time, all of the people were really confused. What was he trying to do?

The point he was making was that there are two ways to communicate: a monologue, like the sermon he was preaching and a conversation, like he was having with the people. He went on to point out that while monologues, like sermons, were fine and useful, they were not nearly as exciting and as intimate a way to communicate as was a good two-way conversation. Then he added that the problem with prayer is that it is a one-way monologue for most of us, and not only are we often bored with it, but Jesus may be bored with it as well. Too often, the great problem with our praying is that we don't

FRIENDSHIP IS LISTENING TO EACH OTHER

give Jesus a chance to talk to us! We do all the talking! We don't listen. We expect Jesus to do all the listening.

But how do we listen to Jesus? How does Jesus talk to us? Does he speak out loud? We have to know how he talks to us if we are going to listen to him. We have to be able to recognize his voice. We've been listening to Jesus by putting a verse in our mind for each of the four previous section of this little book. I hope you have repeated a verse each morning before you got up and then, taking it with you, repeated it often throughout the day and applied it to the incidents of the day. Think about the ways in which Jesus, through these verses, has guided you. Reflect for a few moments, as you start this next section, on exciting answers to your prayers.

One of the greatest problems in friendship is expressed in the statement, *but you are not listening to me!* Teenagers say it to parents. Spouses say it to each other. Friends say it to each other. Not listening is the single greatest reason friendships and relationships fail. It is also the single greatest reason why people talk so much about prayer, but pray so little. We don't know how to listen to Jesus. I hope that you have been practicing listening to Jesus by taking one verse with you daily throughout all the chapters in each section. One verse is enough. You don't need more. The verse needs constant repetition, in order to become part of us.

Listening to Jesus can be done alone, but when we do it as a small group it becomes more dramatic and there is less chance of misinterpreting what he says. I taught a small group of Christians how to pray by drawing pictures of their prayers and then drawing pictures of Jesus' answers. It didn't catch on. But what did catch on was the idea of listening to Jesus through a verse of Scripture. The pastor and a few elders developed the idea of listening to Jesus, as a congregation, by selecting a verse of Scripture that pertained to each decision the congregation had to make at the annual business meeting. At the next congregational meeting the pastor introduced the idea. Instead of discussion and arguing, he said, they would be provided with complete information on the decision they were to make. He would then give the congregation an appropriate verse and they would listen to Jesus speak through it. After a few minutes of listening they were to turn in their vote on a piece of paper. They were amazed at the new unity they found. It was electrifying!

This method of listening spread rapidly upward to district board meetings supervising all 200 churches in the area. When the board was challenged by their denomination to raise $1.3 million dollars for a special missions program, the board refused to vote immediately, but rather meditated on a verse and then turned in on slips of paper the amount of money they thought they should raise. There was no discussion or argument about the suggested amount. When they received all the slips of paper, twenty minutes later, they were overwhelmed – no one voted for the $1.3 million dollars! A new, unanimous figure of $6 million was turned in, without any discussion. Three years later Jesus had provided that amount of money. When a congregation learns how to listen to Jesus by meditating on Scripture prior to making a decision, the fire of the Holy Spirit will descend on the commu-

who do you look like?

nity! In the next chapters we concentrate on floating a phrase of the Lord's Prayer daily, by thinking about it one word or phrase at a time.

Reflect

1. Spend this day reflecting on your favorite verse of Scripture. Apply it to the various challenges and opportunities of the day.

2. At the end of the day, record your experiences.

Prayer

Precious Savior, help me develop the habit of listening to you. I know that the deepening of our friendship depends on more than just you listening to me! Guide me, please, as I keep a verse of your Word in my mind throughout each day. I pray this in your name, Jesus. Amen.

Chapter Twenty-Six

The Position of Prayer

Float this phrase today:
Our Father in heaven… Matthew 6:9 (NIV)

Trusting Jesus as a little child does is so important that when Jesus taught us how to pray, using the outline of the Lord's Prayer, he began at the very point at which a child would begin, addressing God as our Father in heaven. A child is secure, because at a young age, she knows that she is surrounded by a loving family. Think of the sign on heaven's door as saying, *Only Children Admitted! Jesus called a small child over to him and put the child among them. Then he said, I assure you, unless you turn from your sins and become as little children, you will never get into the Kingdom of Heaven. Therefore, anyone who becomes as humble as this little child is the greatest in the Kingdom of Heaven* (Matthew 18:3-4).

who do you look like?

Float this phrase in your mind for an entire day. *Our Father in heaven.* Run those four words over and over in your mind. Start with the word *Our. Our* means family and family means belonging; being surrounded by loving people. Those who believe in Jesus are part of his worldwide family. We have a place; we belong. Brothers and sisters who care for us and pray for us surround us if we are in a Bible believing church. We should be in a small group or Sunday School class to fully experience this, for being in a large worship service seldom provides us with the emotional certainty of knowing that we belong to our faithful Savior Jesus Christ's family here on earth. We *are* part of a family. Think about that today.

Next, concentrate on the word *Father*. Children are dependent creatures. They cannot care for themselves. They need parents to protect them, feed them, clothe them, provide them with housing, and train them to grow up. While never taught dependency, children are dependent creatures by nature. Adults, by nature, are independent. To be saved, we need two conversions: one from sin,

THE POSITION OF PRAYER

and the other from being independent to having a childlike dependency on Jesus. Like little children who become very frightened when they are out of the presence of their loving and caring parents, we become frightened when we are out of touch with Jesus.

Adults are independent, relying on their own skills and talents to solve their problems. It is hard for them to depend on Jesus like a little child. Jesus said that we must change from having an adult self-dependency to having a childlike trust, which is evidenced by our depending on him for all of our needs. Put it this way: You are either S-D or C-D. You are either self-dependent or Christ-dependent. Only those who trust in Jesus like little children will enter heaven.

Jesus said that we are to have a childlike trust and are to be blissfully happy trusting that he will protect and provide for us. This is living in the position of prayer. This is the foundation on which all prayer rests. This comes from knowing that we have a Father in heaven. This Father is the greatest of all fathers. He is the person who has not only created

who do you look like?

all things, but he also sustains everything. Whenever I see a mountain I think, *That's what my Father made, and I am his child!* All the scenes of nature remind me both of his beauty and of his power. I always am overwhelmed then, to think that this God, this Holy Spirit, dwells in me and makes me his sanctuary.

In 1 Thessalonians 5:16-18 Paul tells us, *Be joyful always; pray continually; give thanks in all circumstances* (NIV). If prayer were limited to asking God for things, it would be impossible to pray continually, for we would never be able to do anything else but be asking! We would be talking to God all the time and that would get very boring, both for us and also for Jesus! Jesus would like to say something occasionally too! There is more to prayer than talking to Jesus. Prayer is a position of childlike trust and dependency. Dependency is an attitude, just as being joyful and being grateful is. I don't always have to say, *I'm so happy!* to *be* happy all the time, nor do I have to constantly say, *Thank you* in order to have a grateful heart. These are attitudes. So too, I don't always have to have my eyes closed and be talking to God to be in prayer. Prayer is being like a little child, filled with joy, gratitude and a quiet, careful trust that its loving parents will supply all its needs. Most of the time, children are not even aware of their trust in their parents. It is natural to them.

Here are three of the many ways Jesus will speak to us. He will give us:

<u>An instinct to help</u>. Childlike dependence on Jesus will make us act instinctively to help others. Often adults first measure the cost of helping others, while children do not wait, but instead act instinctively and immediately. When we see people in need, we will respond naturally and immediately to the Holy Spirit's inner prompting to help that person, just as a little child would act. This is one of the most important and powerful forms of wordless prayer. It is God's Holy Spirit moving within us.

<u>A distinct impulse to act</u>.

A more direct way of hearing God than acting instinctively is to receive a distinct thought. Sometimes we will awaken in the night with a special burden for a friend. Sometimes we will have an urge to call someone. We must listen to the Lord

who do you look like?

and act on these thoughts. A good friend of mine, Clare De Graaf, has written an excellent little book, *The Ten Second Rule*. In it he shows how the Spirit prompts us through impulses and we should obey them within ten seconds. Before we begin any major project, we should wait in prayer, asking God to show us his plan, rather than asking him to bless ours. One of the greatest positions to be in is the position of not knowing what to do! It gives you the opportunity to be free from your own plans and to wait until God clearly opens up the door.

<u>Instructions for the moment</u>.

Float a verse of Scripture in your mind each day. Jesus guides us to Scripture verses that give comfort, strength or guidance for the specific need of the moment. By reciting the same verse daily for an entire week that verse becomes part of us. Thinking according to the verse becomes a habit. Jesus instructs us in every situation throughout the day!

Reflect

1. What sign is over heaven's door? (Matthew 18:3)

THE POSITION OF PRAYER

2. Dependency is the primary characteristic of a child. Have you ever been child-like in prayer?

3. When we cultivate childlike dependency we are in the position of prayer. Why is this a good position to hear God speak to us?

4. What are three of the many ways God speaks to us:

Prayer

Give us that childlike joy, peace, and gratitude that comes from a carefree trusting in you, Jesus. How we praise you that you care for us so much that you have counted the number of hairs on our head and are concerned when so much as one of them falls out. May we go through each day living in this quiet confidence and trust in you. In your name we pray. Amen.

Chapter Twenty-Seven

Prayer Begins with Praise

Float this phrase today:
*... hallowed be your name, your kingdom come,
your will be done on earth as it is in heaven.*
Matthew 6:9-10 (NIV)

The position of childlike trust and its resulting carefree, joy-filled, grateful spirit, is called praise. Praise in prayer is as necessary as a wick is to a candle. Unless one lights the wick, the candle will not burn and give light. Unless we fill our prayers with praise, they will not ascend. Praise is the wings of prayer which lift our prayers to the Lord.

I have prayed many times only to become more discouraged and depressed than I was before I began. I could never understand why, until one day I realized that when I prayed, I was concentrating only on my problems and not on my Savior. I was not in a childlike position of total trust. Instead, I was reviewing my difficulties, feeling sorry for myself, and becoming overwhelmed with the fact that I could not solve my problems. Because I did not see any solution for my problems, I didn't think God could either. When I ended a prayer, I was depressed. I was not trusting Jesus to take care of the problem. I demanded to know how he would do it, and I lacked the childlike trust that Jesus would answer in ways I could not imagine. My prayers were not first of all an expression of love to God, but instead were primarily concerned with my needs and solving my problems.

Friendship grows in proportion to the way we express our love and appreciation for each other. If a friend cannot get beyond self-pity to appreciate the other friend, the friendship dies. All friendship is built on a mutual exchange of concern for each other. Politeness is showing concern for each other. We start conversations by saying, *How have*

who do you look like?

you been? or *What's up?* These are ways of showing our interest in our friends and saying that they are important to us. We want to know what's happening in their lives. In this prayer, Jesus tells us to start our prayer by concentrating first on showing our interest in him. We must show him that we are concerned with honoring his name, the coming of his kingdom, and the doing of his will. In a friendship, if we constantly lament about how hard we have it, showing only concern for ourselves and none for our friends, friendships become one-way streets. True friends are mutually concerned for each other. Jesus teaches us to be concerned for our Father's concerns before we bring our own concerns.

Praise is showing our concern for God, and it is just as necessary as showing concern for our friends. If our prayers begin and end with our lists of personal needs, and we spend no time in thanks for what God has done, we fail to light the wick of prayer. Prayer is more than expressing our concern for ourselves; it must also express concern for God—for the honor of his name, the coming of his kingdom and the doing of his will.

PRAYER BEGINS WITH PRAISE

Hallowed be your name. Jesus tells us to start praying with concern for God's desires—for the honor of his name, the coming of his kingdom and the doing of his will. These opening three petitions of the prayer which Jesus gave us show us the polite way to start a conversation with our heavenly Father.

Praise is more than thoughts or songs, however. We praise God by our deeds and by our requests that his name be honored, his kingdom come, and his will be done. When we back up these requests with our work to hallow God's name, bring his kingdom, and do his will, we are praising God. Praise is more than singing or words. It is doing God's will; doing God's will is just as much a prayer as are words.

Names in the Bible describe God. The name *Father*, with which Jesus starts this prayer, describes God's provision and protection. *Emmanuel* confirms that God is with us at all times. *Lord, God Almighty*, tells us that God is the Lord of all the earth, and he is all powerful. The *Good Shepherd* describes Jesus' activity in caring for us. You may find a list of God's names in any good study Bible. Float one or two of them in your mind, recalling

who do you look like?

them frequently throughout the day, and seeing all the things that happen in the light of those names. That's part of what it means to hallow God's name.

We long for the good name of our loved ones to be honored, and this is also important in our relationship with God. The third of the Ten Commandments says, *You shall not misuse the name of the Lord your God* (Exodus 20:7). When we pray that God's names be hallowed, we are praising him by our desire that God always be respected. We are saying that we love him so much that we want everyone to love him and refer to him with respect and love, never taking his precious name in vain. This is praise—not only to desire but also to do something so that everyone may know who God is and to respect him by treating all of his characteristics with reverence and awe.

Our lives must be filled with excitement about God—about his love, his purity, his power, his compassion and his forgiveness in Jesus. It must show in our worship, in our singing, and in all aspects of our lives. One poet put it this way: *May my whole being and my ways, in every part, be filled with praise.*

Your Kingdom come. Jesus came to establish his Father's rule over the world. Our Father's Kingdom is one where everyone will be equal. All will be treated justly and with love. It is a Kingdom in which there will never be any lying or stealing. People will not hurt each other or hate God. Satan and all the devils will be completely destroyed. Sickness and death will be no more. Sadness and sorrow will be gone, and there will be eternal joy. Feeling excitement about this kingdom and working for its establishment are forms of praise. Remember that God's kingdom will come on a new, re-created earth. There will be no need for the sun for Christ himself will live with us on this earth. *And there will be no night there—no need for lamps or sun—for the Lord God will shine on them. And they will reign forever and ever* (Revelation 22:5)

Your will be done on earth as it is in heaven. The beauty of heaven lies in the fact that there is only *one will* in heaven, and everyone agrees on it. No one quarrels or argues in heaven, for there is nothing about which to quarrel. Everyone is agreed—our Father's will is the best! The will of our

who do you look like?

Father is for us to give generously and to love God above all and to love our neighbors as ourselves. Heaven is when everyone agrees that our Father's will is best. To live this way is to live in praise to God and, thus, to live in constant prayer.

We must start our prayers by praising God first. Praise is showing our concern for his names, his kingdom, and his will. The foundation of prayer lies in having a childlike trust in God that leads to an active concern for our Father's name, kingdom and will; this is the highest form of praise.

As you go through the day, float this opening statement in your mind. Ask Jesus to enable you to honor God's name, to bring his kingdom, and to do his will in every part of the day. Listen as he guides you. Live the day in praising him in these three areas.

Reflect

1. How do we show courtesy and politeness when we begin a conversation?

2. The first three petitions of the Lord's Prayer

express our courtesy by being concerned about the honor of His name. How do you begin your prayers as you begin a conversation with the Lord?

3. What is the function of God's names?

4. What does it mean to hallow God's name?

5. What are we praying for when we pray for the coming of God's kingdom?

6. What is the *will* of God?

Prayer

Precious Savior, grant that every part of our lives might be filled with praise. Grant that our childlike trust and carefree attitude may give rise to constant praise. May we never be so concerned about ourselves that we fail to be concerned about the hallowing of your name, the coming of your kingdom, and the doing of your will. For Jesus' sake, we pray. Amen.

Chapter Twenty-Eight

Provision

*Our Father in heaven,
Hallowed be your name, Your kingdom come,
Your will be done on earth as it is in heaven.*

Float this phrase today:
Give us this day our daily bread ...
Matthew 6:9-11(NIV)

Having expressed our concern for our heavenly Father, Jesus now tells us to express our concerns and needs to our Father. We are polite and courteous in our prayer when we begin in concern for our Father. This politeness is a form of praise. We praise God by longing for his characteristics to be respected, and his kingdom to be established and his will to be done everywhere.

It is in that context of praise that we now present our needs to him. Just as a good, but imperfect, earthly father is concerned about his children's needs, so much more is our perfect heavenly Father concerned about all our needs. Jesus said, *You parents—if your children ask for a loaf of bread, do you give them a stone instead? Or if they ask for a fish, do you give them a snake? Of course not! If you sinful people know how to give good gifts to your children, how much more will your heavenly Father give good gifts to those who ask him?* (Matthew 7:9-11)

When it comes to earthly needs, we have three problems. The first and greatest problem is that we do not know what our real needs are. Like little children, we may want to touch a hot stove and our mommy, in love, slaps our hand and pulls it away to protect us. The second problem is that we think we must supply those needs through our own efforts and that we don't need our Father. The third problem is that we want our needs solved in our own way, and when God takes another way, we get angry. Satan uses our shortcomings to make us doubt God. We must always remember God's promises to meet all of our needs. Here are some of those promises.

who do you look like?

Philippians 4:19: *And this same God who takes care of me will supply all your needs from his glorious riches, which have been given to us in Christ Jesus.* While this promise is certainly for everyone, it is especially meaningful to those who live in poverty. There are three key concepts to meditate on throughout the day.

• First, *God* will meet our needs. We must trust him, as a child trusts its parents. God is infinitely wealthy. Our Father in heaven not only owns all, but he is all-powerful. When the kings of Israel trusted God, God always delivered them. God has given two great pictures of deliverance in the Old Testament: first when he parted the Red Sea so that the Israelites could escape from the Egyptians, and second, when he parted the Jordan River to allow the Israelites to enter the Promised Land.

• The second concept in this verse involves the word *needs*. God does not promise to give us everything we *want*. Sometimes when God answers our prayers and gives us what we need, it is something that we do not want; however, he knows that we need it desperately in order to prepare us for heaven. It is important to realize that this life is a school that is preparing us for eternal life, and we have many important lessons to learn. Some of these lessons include suffering and hardship as the only way to mature us (James 1:2-4).

• The third concept in this verse is the idea that God's provision for us is measured by his glorious riches in Christ Jesus. God will provide for our needs far beyond all the limits of our imaginations (Ephesians 3:20).

Matthew 18:19 (NIV): *Again, I tell you that if two of you on earth agree about anything you ask for, it will be done for you by my Father in heaven.*

This is a unique promise of provision that is often misunderstood. There is special power in prayer when two or more of us agree on something. Some object to this, saying that it teaches that we can get God to change his mind if more than one person prays. In other words, God responds to the *pressure* of many praying.

We have fifteen grandchildren. If just one of them asks us to do something, we certainly will listen, but if all fifteen come to us, surround us, hold hands, and ask us as their grandma and grandpa to do something, we will surely give special attention to that request. There is a special delight that our Father has when we join hands together in unity and love, and as his family members, unite together in prayer. This is not extra pressure but is simply a powerful expression of love and unity.

<u>John 15:16, 17</u>: *You did not choose me, but I chose you...to go and bear fruit—fruit that will last. Then the Father will give you whatever you ask in my name. This is my command: love each other.* (NIV)

In this verse we see the condition on which our requests for provision will be granted. We can ask for whatever we need *in order to bear much fruit*, and the Father will grant it as long as we ask for it in the name of the One who lives in us. The fruit that Christ wants us to bear is explained and summarized: love God above all else and love one another as you love yourself. God will give us *anything* we need in order to enable us to love!

Reflect

1. According to Matthew 7:9-11, how can we be absolutely certain that our Father in heaven will meet all our needs?

2. According to Philippians 4:19, to what *extent* will God meet our needs? Explain the meaning of this phrase.

3. Why does God take special delight when two or more people gather for prayer? Are these prayers more *effective* than the prayers of a single person? What is different about them?

4. For what reason, according to John 15:16-17, will God answer our prayers?

5. Explain the difference between what we *want* and what we *need*. Give examples of how what we want can be pleasant at first, but painful in the end. Give examples of how what we need might be painful at first, but good for us in the end.

who do you look like?

Prayer

Thank you, Savior for encouraging us to ask our Father to fill all our needs. As you live in us, and as you have made us your branches, your body, and your building, please fill us with all we need to be powerful instruments of your love. In your name we pray, Jesus. Amen.

Chapter Twenty-Nine

Prayers for Peace

*Our Father in heaven,
hallowed be your name, your kingdom come, your
will be done on earth as it is in heaven.
Give us today our daily bread.*

Float this phrase today:
*Forgive us our debts, as we also have forgiven our
debtors.* Matthew 6:9-12 (NIV)

Debt. Now that is a familiar word. Most of us, carry a mountain of debt on our backs. Credit card debt, mortgage debt, car loans... it all adds up in painful mountains. In India debt among the poor is even worse. One of the greatest problems in India's economy is that of the loan sharks who prey on the poor. Since at least 40% of India's people cannot read or write, they are easy prey for crooked loans.

who do you look like?

Loan sharks will tell the people one thing, and then they will write something else in the contract. The illiterates sign with a fingerprint, not knowing what the loan shark has actually written in the loan, and most of the time, they sign themselves to loans they cannot possibly repay. The loan shark demands the interest payment weekly or monthly and beats them if they cannot pay it. They become virtual slaves.

That's what debt is, in a way. It is slavery. It is giving away our freedom. Debt is not merely financial—it is another word for sin. When we owe someone something and refuse to pay it, we sin. We have stolen from them by not repaying what we owe, and until the debt is paid, there will be no peace. We cannot have a decent friendship when we refuse to repay a debt. A friend of mine loaned another believer several thousand dollars to help him out during a crisis in his life. Ten years later the friend had not even tried to repay it, and tension filled their relationship. The friend often reminded the borrower of the loan, and finally, in great irritation, the debtor said that he did not intend ever to pay it back! He terminated the friendship by refusing to repay the debt.

In a sense, all we have is a loan from God. The very fact that we have life is a gift from God. Everyone is a gift of God. The flowers, the sun, the lakes, and the birds and animals, all are God's gifts. The ability to love someone is a gift. Parents who care for us are gifts of God. When God created the first humans, Adam and Eve, he gave them to each other. When he first created Adam, he said, *It is not good for the man to be alone. I will make a companion who will help him* (Genesis 2:18). God made a woman, Eve, and gave her to Adam, and the gift of friendship was born.

With all these gifts God gives, he has a right to receive something from us in return. Friendship is a mutual caring for each other. When friendship consists of only one friend giving to another, without any return, this is parasitism. When we become parasites, sucking all we can from others, without any compassion or concern for them, we kill friendship. This is exactly what is wrong with our society today—greed sours everything. When we look at others only in terms of what we can get from them, we build our own debt, which is sin!

This is why Jesus calls sin debt. We are to ask forgiveness for our debt to God. But how can we be forgiven, if we owe so much to him. Everything about us, everything that defines us—our talents, our lives, and our energy—all is a gift from God. Have you ever thought about this or considered what we owe God? Our entire lifetime is a loan from God that must be paid. This is why Jesus came—he came to pay the debt each of us owes God. And when by faith, Jesus enters us, he covers all our debt to the Father, as we have seen earlier. He has paid it all. Our debt is gone because the One who paid our debt now lives in us! When the Father looks at us he sees his Son in us; he sees the One who have paid the entire debt! We can have true, eternal rest, peace, and freedom when Christ dwells in us.

It is then that we can extend this debt relief to our friends. We all sin not only against God, but we also sin against each other by not repaying the debts we owe. Sin is pure selfishness. Sin is living to get. And when others have sucked everything out of us and fail to repay, relationships break down. This is especially true in marriage when one spouse makes demands on the other and never considers his or her own obligations. Forgiveness from God is debt relief and forgiveness to others is also debt relief. Failure to forgive debt is a burden eating at both parties, the one owed and the one who owes. If I have someone who has failed to pay me back for some good thing I gave to them, it can eat at me like a cancer. Peace has two aspects; it consists of knowing that my debt with God is cancelled, but it also involves knowing that I have canceled others' debts to me.

This, of course, is not possible in our human strength. But when Jesus lives in us, he fills us so full that we don't need anything else. What others owe us is nothing now, for we are full of the Savior. We cannot hold anything more, and thus we need not hold on to what others owe us, but instead we can freely forgive them. This is why Jesus linked God's forgiveness of our debt to our forgiving the debts that others owe us. We can only do this when we realize that we are filled with the infinite, unlim-

who do you look like?

ited gifts of the presence of Jesus and need nothing more.

Reflect

1. Make a list of all the gifts God has given you. Think about what you owe him.

2. Make a list of what you have given to others.

3. Are there those who have not given back? Ask Jesus to give you the fullness and awareness of his paying your debt, so that in that peace, you can forgive the debts of others.

Prayer

Precious Savior, please help me to see the great debt I owe you, and the impossibility of ever paying you back for all your goodness to me. Then help me trust that you, yourself, have paid it all back to our heavenly Father for me, and that I am now debt free for eternity. In that joy, peace and freedom, enable me to set free all those who still owe me something. Grant that I may forgive them. For your sake, Jesus, I pray. Amen.

Chapter Thirty

Prohibiting Prayers

*Our Father in heaven, hallowed be your name,
your kingdom come, your will be done
on earth as it is in heaven.
Give us today our daily bread.
Forgive us our debts, as we also have
forgiven our debtors.
And lead us not into temptation, but deliver us
from evil… Matthew 6:9-13(NIV)*

Float this verse today:
*Whatever you bind on earth will be bound in
heaven… Matthew 18:18 (NIV)*

Several years ago I was involved in an exhausting speaking tour. For four weeks I conducted a day-long seminar, each day in a different city. I travelled from one city to another at night. I returned

PROHIBITING PRAYERS

home for weekends, but on the final weekend I was so exhausted that when I returned home, I lay down on the sofa and stared at the ceiling, saying nothing, until nearly midnight.

Finally my wife knelt beside me and quietly started to pray. Suddenly I sat bolt upright! I asked her what she was doing, and she replied, *I was prohibiting Satan and his demons from bothering you*. The change in my emotions was one of the most dramatic, most sudden, transformations I have ever experienced. The demonic entity that had attacked me, sensing my extreme weariness as his opportunity, was prohibited from operating any more by my wife's prayer. This spirit recognized the authority of Jesus, who lives in my wife. As that spirit was bound, I went from the depths of weariness to the heights of thankful praise!

We had another similar experience a few years later. I left for work one morning in deep depression. During the day, the depression mysteriously left. When I returned home that evening, I walked up to the house whistling and singing, something I rarely do. My wife greeted me at the door with a

who do you look like?

big smile, and I asked her what she had done during the day. She told me that she had spent the day fasting and praying that the evil one would leave me alone. Once again, she had prohibited demonic spirits from attacking me by using the authority and power of the One who lives in her. The change in my condition was nothing short of supernatural. In both of these instances, she was acting as part of God's police force. In the authority of Christ, who dwells in her, and clothed with the uniform of prayer, she was arresting evil spirits.

As disciples of Jesus, we must be aware of two things. First, Satan and his demons are constantly watching and waiting for times to attack us with temptation. Second, Jesus teaches us to pray, after having been forgiven, that we not only be spared these attacks but also, if they do come, that we prohibit or forbid the demonic powers to conquer us. It is most appropriate to pray for deliverance from the evil one and his legions. Jesus himself taught us to do this. In Luke 9:1 we are told, *One day Jesus called together his twelve apostles and gave them power and authority to cast out demons and to heal diseases.* We have included *prohibition* as one of the powers of prayer. This is the power of prohibiting the activity of the evil one in our lives through the presence and authority of Christ who lives in us.

The meaning of *lead us not into temptation* is this. There are various situations in life in which we are especially vulnerable to demonic attack. While it is a blessing to go through them victoriously, it is not wrong to ask our heavenly Father, for Jesus' sake, to excuse us from them. And, when we are in them, we are to wear the uniform of Christ's police force—the uniform of prayer in the name of Jesus. Jesus is in charge of our lives, and he leads us. At times, as the Father did with his own Son, he will allow us to enter a battlefield with demonic power. This is called temptation. *Then Jesus was led out into the wilderness by the Spirit to be tempted there by the devil* (Matthew 4:1). Jesus was led by the Holy Spirit into battle with Satan. It was an agonizing time. It was so exhausting for our Lord that at the end *angels came and cared for Jesus.* (Matthew 4:11). God will also test us from time to time. These are exhausting battles. Paul tells us that we wrestle not

who do you look like?

with flesh and blood, but with principalities and powers (Ephesians 6:12).

Here are some examples of our spiritual battlegrounds.

<u>Poverty</u>. The constant, wearisome, daily grind of not having enough money or food is a favorite opportunity for demonic powers to lead us into the sin of bitterness or other sins, such as stealing or selling our bodies in order to get enough food. Jesus teaches us to plead, for his sake, that we be delivered from poverty. He also gives us authority to prohibit the demonic powers from afflicting us when we are poor by binding them in his name (Matthew 18:18). Jesus also teaches us that the way out of poverty is to tithe! (Malachi 3:10)

<u>Persecution</u>. While persecution may be necessary for revitalizing the disciples of Jesus, it can also be very dangerous. God is using persecution in India to light fires of revival, but at the same time, there are casualties in this spiritual battle. Some will fall away from following the Savior. Demonic power can be very active in times of persecution. It is right to pray for freedom from persecution, but we must also prohibit the evil spirits from working

in times of persecution by praying for deliverance from them.

Pain. Chronic illness, disability, and continuous pain are also opportunities both for experiencing the tremendous power of God and for experiencing discouragement and a feeling of a lack of faith. Paul pleaded with God to take away his mysterious disability, but God refused (2 Corinthians 12:9). Paul lived with this challenge for many years, and his faith and trust in God only increased.

Prosperity. Perhaps the most dangerous battleground, the one in which demonic powers are most successful, is material prosperity. When we become wealthy, we tend to trust our money and our talents rather than God, and we can wander very far from him.

Many of the newer translations eliminate the word *one* (evil one) and merely use the word evil. However, there is ample reason to use *evil one*. When Christ dwells within us, he brings into our being his authority over the *evil ones* or demonic spirits. He gives us the right to invoke this authority by rebuking them in his name. Deliverance from evil, from the *evil one* and *evil ones,* is based

who do you look like?

on Colossians 2:15 (NIV): *And having disarmed the powers and authorities [evil ones], he made a public spectacle of them, triumphing over them by the cross.* Our Lord has disarmed and humiliated the demonic hosts; that very same Lord lives in us! Christians who do not use the power and authority of the One who lives in them in their spiritual battle with evil, open themselves to incredible attacks and crippling spiritual weakness.

The problems of inner city slums plague our urban areas. Violence, child abuse, gangs, and sexual crimes abound. Yet Christians also inhabit these cities. However, these Christians do not understand that since Christ lives in them, they are now God's police force, given Christ's authority to rebuke demonic powers, arrest them, and demolish the strongholds of lies, which they create. As the Good News sweeps through developing countries, the new Christians are far more aware of their value and power in Christ than older, Western Christians seem to be. During the twentieth century, disciples in the developing countries, including India, have made more disciples of Christ than the total number made, world-wide, in the previous nineteen hundred years! These *first-faith* believers do not need training to understand their authority over evil spirit beings. They have lived in bondage to them. They know their reality. And when the Holy Spirit dwells for the first time in the new believers, they know that they have a power over these evil spirits.

Prayer begins with childlike trust and moves into childlike praise and adoration for our Father in heaven. It continues with a simple trust that all our needs will be met, and that the measure by which they are met is the riches of Christ Jesus. The fourth dimension in prayer deals with the forgiveness of our debts (sins) and our ability to forgive those who have sinned against us. The fifth dimension of prayer deals with the authority and power of Christ who lives in us to prohibit demonic activity in our lives. As we realize who lives in us, we will grow in our power to exercise his authority and power against the demonic spirits, which constantly attempt to lead us into sin.

who do you look like?

Reflect

1. How do you explain Ephesians 6:12?

2. Do you believe that demons attack Christians? Can you give any illustrations?

3. What are some common battlefields in which we wage war with demonic powers? Give some examples additional to those given in the lesson.

4. Why does God allow this spiritual warfare to go on (James 1:1-4)?

5. Who is Christ, according to Colossians 2:15?

6. Since Christ is in us, what does this mean for us when we engage in spiritual warfare?

7. Is it permissible to pray for escape from spiritual warfare? Answer this in the light of 1 Corinthians 10:13.

Prayer

Savior, forgive us for failing to use your power to rebuke the evil one. Lord, we have unnecessarily allowed the evil one entrance into our lives. Holy Spirit, empower us to prohibit the presence of these evil spirits and thus enable us to live more victoriously. In your name, Jesus, we pray. Amen.

Chapter Thirty-One

Prayer is the Presence of Christ

*Our Father in heaven,
hallowed be your name, your kingdom come,
your will be done on earth as it is in heaven.
Give us this day our daily bread.
Forgive us our debts as we forgive our debtors.
And lead us not into temptation, but deliver us
from the evil one.*

Float this phrase today:
*For yours is the kingdom, the power and the glory
forever, Amen.* Matthew 6:9-15 (NIV)

Again, I tell you that if two of you on earth agree about anything you ask for, it will be done for you by my Father in heaven. For where two or three come together in my name, there I am with them (Matthew 18:19-20).

I took a number of American pastors into a Hindu temple in India. It was the first time any of them had visited such a temple, and the short tour left them shaken. As we left, all of them felt burdened and depressed. On the bus ride back to Chennai they shared their experiences. As they were talking I noticed a small village along the road ahead. I asked if they would like to stop and walk through it. They all agreed, so we stopped the bus, got out and walked into the village. As we entered the village, I told them that I could sense the presence of Christ in the village. Since I had never been in the village, they were a little skeptical and asked how I could tell. One of the physical signs was the neatness and cleanliness there, but there also seemed to be a soft, spiritual atmosphere. We heard singing as we walked into the village. Hidden at the back of the village, we found a church and a Christian school. Boys and girls were singing familiar hymns. The contrast between the feelings we had experienced in the temple and those that we felt in the village was amazing.

who do you look like?

Christ blesses geographic areas with his presence when two or more gather to worship and pray. Some close friends began work in a government housing project, which was riddled with violence and averaged about 15 police calls per day. Some elderly women from a neighboring church wanted to know how they could help. They were asked to pray for the project. They took the challenge seriously, and once a week they gathered in their church, directing their prayers to the project for an hour or two. God answered so dramatically that the number of police calls that summer dropped from 15 a day to about 15 for the remainder of that year!

God blesses geographic areas like slums and specific villages and even temple areas, when we claim them for him through prayer. God will bless houses, shops, factories, school buildings, and even entire states when two or more people are meeting to pray for the area. This is why Project Philip is sponsoring a *County by County* attempt to saturate every zip code area in the United States with prayer and to sow the seed of an overview of God's Word in those homes. This, more than any other activity, will release the supernatural, transforming power of God on our nation.

Normally when coming to Kolkata (Calcutta), India, I experience heavy spiritual oppression. There was one day that was an exception. Arriving in the airport, I felt light-hearted and full of praise. After some time, I became aware of the fact that on this particular day millions of people around the world were praying specifically for this city. I could feel the presence of Christ there in a new and powerful way. I checked into a little hotel in the center of the city and was told upon check-in that some people were waiting for me in an upstairs room. I was surprised, since I thought no one knew I was staying at this hotel. I went upstairs and found a group of American and Canadian Christians, gathered in prayer, in keeping with the world-wide day of prayer for Kolkata, and the hotel clerk had assumed that I was one of that party.

The Lord's Prayer ends with a doxology, *For Yours is the kingdom, the power and the glory, forever.* While it may be doubtful that Jesus actually included this hymn of praise in his prayer (that's why you won't

who do you look like?

find it in most of Bible translations), it is commonly accepted that he expected this hymn to be added, since it was the custom of his day for followers to sing it, and it is a marvelous summary of the prayer.

Christ claims that everything, every place, and every person belongs to him. As we gather in family devotions, in small prayer cells, and in group worship, we must claim the physical areas in which we meet for Jesus, so that the kingdom, the power, and the glory of Jesus may be shown in them. Jesus promises that he will be present in a special way where two or three are gathered in his name. I believe that he blesses all who are within specific geographic areas with his presence when people are praying for those areas. Let us pray Christ's presence—his kingdom, his power, and his glory—into our fields, shops, schools, neighborhoods, villages, cities, states, and nations!

PRAYER IS THE PRESENCE OF CHRIST

Reflect

1. Share experiences you have had both with feeling the presence of a good and peaceful spirit in a place, and with feeling the presence of a frightening, dark, demonic spirit.

2. Why are new believers in eastern countries more sensitive to spiritual warfare and demonic spirits than older, western believers?

Prayer

*Precious Savior, hear our prayers.
Fill not only this room, but also our
entire neighborhoods, our schools,
our places of work, our homes,
and our stores with your peaceful
presence. In your name, we pray.
Amen.*

♡ Love

Do I look like Love (Christ is love)?

Who do you look like? Jesus is the ultimate picture of acceptance, of hope, and of friendship. Jesus modeled perfect acceptance of sinners. He gave hope to the hopeless. He is the world's greatest friend. Since he lives in us he is our constant companion, speaking to us continuously through the Bible. What did people see in Jesus? They saw someone who accepted them, gave them hope, and offered them friendship. To have Jesus present in us through his Holy Spirit, means that these three great characteristics will shine out of us. When we accept and forgive those who have hurt us, when hope fills us and we encourage the hopeless, when we are friends with others because Christ is our friend, then Christ shines out of us.

The most important characteristic, love, is the last one that we will consider. When people see Jesus, they see love in the form of acceptance, hope and friendship. However, when we talk about love, we immediately confront a problem. <u>Just what does it</u>

mean to love? We use the word to describe a good restaurant—I just love McDonalds. We describe sex as making love. We speak about loving pets; loving school; loving friends; loving candy; and loving golf, bowling, basketball, soccer, and fishing! We use the word, love, so widely that it is one of the most confusing of all English words! Love, as Jesus used the word and illustrated it in his life, is the greatest attribute we are to demonstrate. It is good, then, to define his kind of love. That is what we are now going to do in this final set of meditations.

If Christ lives in us, then his love must be shining out of us, unless we have our shades pulled down! If we are living for self, and are not concerned about others, we have pulled the drapes and closed the windows of our heart! If we are to look like Jesus, because Jesus lives in us, then our goal must be to let his love, his acceptance, his hope and his friendship show in all of our conduct and character.

Open your shades and let Christ's light radiate through you!

Float this verse daily as you study Part Six.
But now abides faith, hope and love and the greatest of these is love.
1 Corinthians 13:13 (NIV)

Chapter Thirty-Two

Loving is Giving Life

I am giving you a new commandment: love each other! John 13:34

Over and over the Bible emphasizes the importance of love. The greatest commandments are to love God above all else and to love our neighbors as ourselves. Jesus said that everyone would know that we are his disciples by the love we display. God created us as male and female so that our love relationship would reflect God's love relationship between Father, Son and Holy Spirit. In loving each other, we demonstrate that we are living as children who have been made in the image and likeness of God. In a sense, loving is giving life to another, not merely physical life, but emotional and spiritual life as well. When we fall in love, it means that someone has accepted us; we are excited as we anticipate and hope for a bright future.

How valuable is a person who can truly love

someone else? How important is such a person? The highest compliment we can give to another is to say that that person is a loving person. When Jesus lives in us, he transforms us to love. He tells us in John 7:38-39 that whoever believes in him will become the headwaters, or the origin of rivers of living water, which is another symbol for love. Living water is life-giving water. Living water is another word for the love of God flowing out of us. Jesus promised that when love for others flows out of us, life will spring up everywhere, just as when a river flows, green life springs up along its banks.

Jesus defined his disciples in terms of love. *So now I am giving you a new commandment: Love each other. Just as I have loved you, you should love each other. Your love for one another will prove to the world that you are my disciples (John 13:34-35).*

The cover of this book has the picture of masks, suggesting the question, *Who Do We Look Like?* We all live with a mask. We try to hide our true identities. If we are followers of Jesus, and if Jesus lives in us, then we must remove our masks. We are the house in which Jesus dwells. We are his body, his temple, his dwelling place, and his sanctuary.

who do you look like?

The big lie of Satan is to make us believe that our importance comes from our appearance, or our money, or our reputation, or the things we own. Those things are all the things that bring value to a museum! Do you want to go through life as a dusty, lifeless museum? No? Then stop building your self-image on these things. Stop finding your value in your looks and your worldly possessions. You are NOT a museum; you are the home of the King of Kings and the Lord of Lord's. The old you has died. The new you has come. Rejoice and be glad!

When Jesus lives in us, his unique, transforming love must pour out of us, just as light shines out of the windows of a house at twilight. The love of Jesus is supernatural. It is radically different from what we understand love to be. We think of love as an attraction to something or someone. When we say we love candy, we are really saying that we like candy very much. When we say that we love a certain show, we are saying that we like it better than other shows. When we say that we have fallen in love, we are saying that we are attracted to someone; we really like that person. This is not the kind of love that Jesus offers. Jesus' love is the opposite of merely liking someone; it is love that is directed to those we do not even like! It is being genuinely concerned for people who are disgusting to us. It is caring for the unlovable. The kind of love that Jesus shows will often break our hearts by its amazing depths. Before Jesus comes into our hearts, we care only about building our self-image on what we do. To love others is to share in their sorrow and suffering. That is Jesus' love!

A terrorist organization sent a young man to spy on a Children's Bible Club in India. He was a nineteen-year-old radical. The Children's Bible Club was a two-week club, sponsored by Mission India, whose staff trained the volunteers of a local church. The young man carefully watched what was happening in the club. He saw the children laughing as they sang songs he had never heard before. He saw them praying. Most of all, he saw the amazing love of the teachers as they gently cared for each of the little ones there. He came filled with hatred and a desire to disrupt the activities of these Christians. Hatred, hardness, cruelty and suspicion had filled his life up until this time. He was confused.

who do you look like?

The love of Christ flowed from the teachers, embracing every one of the children, especially the most unruly and unattractive. He had never seen anything like it. If you did not like someone, as a terrorist, you eliminated that person; you certainly did not care for the person and help him. What kind of conduct was he seeing? He found that those who had been unruly and unattractive were being loved in the camp, and this love was transforming them and filling them with joy. At the same time, joy also filled the people who did the loving. The rivers of love softly melted his hard heart, and within a few days, the spy opened his heart and the Savior entered. He became a new man in Christ, and the old, cruel person died. He left with the love of Jesus in his heart. He no longer lived (as a terrorist) but Christ came in and lived in him.

This new man in Christ had been a terrorist, and terrorists are trained to act. They do not sit around discussing things. They move. Shortly after coming to Christ and learning more about the Children's Bible Club, he left his terrorist organization and instead organized a Children's Bible Club. He acted rapidly, and in the next year, he organized several more Bible Clubs and trained teachers to organize their own. Within just nine short years, he had organized clubs that reached 35,000 boys and girls with the love of Jesus Christ! Christ's love poured out of him, bringing new life, eternal life, to tens of thousands of children over the years. Previously he never even noticed children, much less loved them, but when Christ took up residence in this young man and made him a sanctuary, Christ's love flowed from him to thousands.

When Christ comes into us, his love transforms us, enabling us to love so much more than merely the things or people we like. In loving the unlovable, the poor, the proud, and the arrogant—in loving (being concerned for) all those who turn us off—we become the head waters of streams of love flowing from us. These streams form many beautiful pools of love: food banks for the hungry; schools for kids that were expelled from regular schools; adoption agencies for homeless orphans; water wells for the thirsty; and hospitals and health clinics for the ill. The list is awesome! As Christ comes into your heart, to make you his dwelling place, you, like that young man and multi-millions of others each year, become the headwaters of torrents of life-giving love that reaches those in desperate need. You move far beyond loving only what you like! You have the love of Christ in you, and you give a radically new, supernatural kind of acceptance, care and friendship to those you would normally just pass by.

Reflect

1. What did you like in this meditation?

2. What is the difference between liking something and loving as Christ loves?

Prayer

Precious Savior, you are the fountain of all love. Place that incredible, infinite, unlimited love in me in so great a measure that it flows from me out to the most difficult and unlovely people in my life, transforming them and bringing them to life. In your name, I pray. Amen.

who do you look like?

Chapter Thirty-Three

The Origin of Love

But God showed his great love for us by sending Christ to die for us while we were still sinners..
Romans 5:8

I will never forget my first impressions of India. I became angry with God when I saw all the poverty, sickness, and despair in that land. I was, to put it mildly, very turned off. I questioned God, asking him why he didn't do something to help all these suffering people. As I asked the question, God put this statement, followed by a question in my mind: *John, I think I have done something. What is it?* The answer came to me immediately. Of course, God has done something, and it is something far greater than all people who have ever lived could ever do. He gave his Son to suffer hell for all of us, including all the persons living in India. He did this amazing act of love, not because he found us so attractive; rather, we are so full of sin that we had to be banished from him forever. He did this because it was the nature of his love. Jesus' love is not pulled out of him by attraction. His is a strange, unique kind of love that is forced out by a power inside of him. It embraces even the most unattractive persons in the world. The Bible repeatedly shows us that God loves us *while we are his enemies.* Jesus' love has caused him more suffering than all the world's suffering combined. I forgot that when I first saw the incredible suffering of the poor in India.

Who has suffered more? Let's put all human suffering together from the time of Adam and Eve, the first people who lived, until today. Sum it all up. Think of all the suffering that the whole human race has endured. Compare that to Jesus' suffering. Who has suffered more? Jesus has! All the suffering of the human race has been temporary suffering. Jesus Christ, suffered eternal punishment for our sins, when he died on Calvary's cross. On that cross he uttered the most profound statement ever heard by human ears, *My God, my God, why have*

who do you look like?

you forsaken me (Matthew 27:46)? In that moment, he finished the eternal punishment for our sins. What would take an eternity for each of us, Christ did in a moment for all of us. We cannot fully understand it, but we can understand that God's suffering for us is infinitely greater than all the suffering that all humans have ever endured, for Jesus bore our eternal punishment for sin.

We often think that Christ's death on the cross was his low point. Actually, what seemed to us to be Christ's low point was really his high point! Suffering forsakenness by the Father on the cross was the highest expression of love ever shown by a human being. After crying out, *My God, why have you forsaken me,* Jesus uttered a sigh of relief as he said, *It is finished* (John 19:30). This means that the punishment for our sins is completely, fully, and eternally paid, and Jesus can flow into us through the presence of his Holy Spirit. We see the true nature of God's love and beauty revealed in the sacrifice of Christ. It is in these pain-filled words that Christ reveals the wonder of his infinite love. What we see as the low point is God's high point! God is not attracted to us by the wonderful deeds we do, and, therefore, loves us for them. God loves us, because of himself, because of who he is. God is love! We base most common forms of love today on attraction. We say we love to sail or sky dive, because we are attracted to these things. The word love is used for so many different objects and persons that it has lost its real meaning. God's love is not based on attraction; we don't pull it out of him by how beautiful we are. God's love is pushed out of him by an internal force to reach out to those who are not attractive to him.

Would you give your life for your friend? Would you ever allow your child to give his life for someone else? Would you allow your child to give his life for your enemy? The Bible tells us that God the Father sent his Son Jesus to die for us *while we were still his enemies* (Romans 5:13)!

In order to release Christ's love in us, we must sacrifice as Christ did. The moment we sacrifice ourselves, we open the floodgates of the water of love, releasing it to flow from us. When Paul said, *I have been crucified with Christ and I no longer live...* (Galatians 2:20), he was stating that it was at the point that his desire to exalt himself was replaced

who do you look like?

with the desire to sacrifice himself for Christ and others, that true love began to flow from him. Even as Christ's love was released by his sacrifice for us, so the rivers of love will be released from us when we sacrifice our lives and desires for others. When Paul said that he was crucified with Christ and he died, he was stating that he had found a new principle for living. He no longer lived selfishly to pursue his own desires. He did not want to exalt himself. He was not trying to reach heights that would make him known by all men. As painful as it might be, he willingly and joyfully set aside all his own desires in order to do what Christ wanted. Loving Christ, not himself, became his joy. When he loved Christ more than himself, he was showing that love by giving himself sacrificially to others.

A young mother had a serious form of cancer. A group of Christian ladies prayed for her healing daily. One day she shared that she had had a dream, and in that dream she saw great streams of people from India pouring into heaven because of her life. The people praying for her thought she would be healed, because God had given her this vision. However, she died a few months later. Five years after her death, a man from India came to her church with a tract. The woman who died had written out her testimony, and it had found its way to India and was printed as a tract. This little pamphlet had been used to plant four churches in India. It had transformed hundreds of lives. Her dream was being fulfilled after she died! This is the wonder of who we are when *Christ lives in us*. The streams of love flowing from us not only last forever, but they continue to multiply and grow, as did this woman's written testimony of her love for Jesus.

Reflect

1. Why can we say that Jesus has suffered infinitely more than the total amount of suffering all humans have endured from creation until today?

2. Explain why Jesus' death on the cross, which seems to be the *low point* of his life and the depth of his suffering, is really the *high point* of God's glorious love. Read Romans 5:6-8.

3. Explain why Christ's death on the cross could release rivers of life-giving love to flow into every nation of the world.

4. Explain why, when we live for ourselves, we shut off rivers of living water, but when we give ourselves in humble service to others, the rivers of water flow.

Prayer

> *Precious Savior, we rejoice that you took on and have perfectly FINISHED all our punishment. We praise you that through your pain and suffering you opened the way to live in us and transform us to be your temples. Grant that as we give ourselves sacrificially to you, we may become the origins of rivers of living water. Thank you, Jesus, for making us to be your life-givers. Show us today where you want the water of life to flow. In your name, we pray. Amen.*

Chapter Thirty-Four

The Direction of Love

*Whoever believes in me, as the Scripture has said…
from within him.… John 7:38*

I have a pencil. You want that pencil. I want your money. We agree that you will give me a certain amount of money for the pencil, and we make the exchange. I give you the pencil; you give me  the money. We are both happy. This is called the equal exchange of value. This equal exchange happens daily all over the world. It happens in the market place, in stores, on computers, and between big companies. It is this constant, equal exchange of goods and services that builds relationships. Conversely, the absence of equal exchange ruins

who do you look like?

relationships. When someone gets something from you and intentionally cheats you by not giving something you feel is equal in exchange, that person has stolen from you.

All relationships are built on mutual exchange: both give, and both parties receive from each other. Loving unions are set up in marriages when both parties are giving and receiving equally. Persons who merely want to receive, or get things, without giving anything back, are parasites, sucking the life out another person. Stealing is against the law everywhere; in some cultures you can have your hands cut off if you are caught robbing another. Equal exchange is a universal, moral law in all religions.

In John 4, we find the story of Jesus walking through Samaria, which was the inner city slum area to the Jews. He rested at a well, and a woman was there drawing water. She was a Samaritan, a kind of untouchable person to the Jews. Jesus asked her for a drink of water, and in doing so, shocked and surprised her. How could a man treat her with this kind of dignity, not only talk to her, but also to ask her for a favor? Have you realized that one of the greatest kindnesses we can give to someone is to ask them for help? It puts us on that person's level; no, it really puts them up a notch above us. We need them. We need their help. In needing their help, we are dignifying them and giving them a precious gift, the gift of being wanted.

I have a friend who operated his business on the principle of dignifying the help by asking them to help him run the business, since they were the ones doing the daily work. He was in the bus business and bought many bus companies servicing airports. One of the first things he did upon acquiring an airport bus company was to get the drivers together to tell them that they were the ones who knew how to run the company, and he was depending upon their suggestions to make it a success. You can imagine what that did to their self-esteem—he valued them!

The Bible tells us that while there is only one God, he exists as three, equal but distinct Persons—Father, Son, and Holy Spirit. While we cannot fully understand this, there is an aspect of it

who do you look like?

that we can understand. These three Persons live in perfect love for each other. They are always giving and receiving equally, and, hence, they exist in perfect harmony. They are constantly giving to each other—the flow is outward from the Father to the Son and the Spirit. Jesus, the Son, loves the Father and the Spirit and sacrifices for them. The Spirit flows outward in bringing glory to the Son and to the Father. As they give to each other, they also then receive from each other. The Triune God is the highest example of giving and receiving. The Triune God is a perfect giving and receiving relationship.

When God created the angels, he made them to be ministering spirits. In other words, they existed to give to God, to each other, and to us, as well. Demons are fallen angels. A fallen angel is one who has stopped the flow of giving. A demon is like a parasite which exists only to suck the life out of other things. Satan no longer wanted to give anything to God. All he wanted, was everything God had, and he wanted it for himself. Satan got twisted and wanted only to receive or get without ever giving. Instead of serving God, he wanted to become God and have all the angels and God serve him. He wanted to occupy the highest place, so that everyone would give to him. He denied that the highest place was the place God occupied, the place of giving the most. He wanted all others to pour their gifts into him. He changed the direction of the flow from selfless service to others to selfish demands that all others serve him, including God.

In a sense, Satan became a half-circle. He cut himself off from all unity and harmony. He could not be with God and the other angels, since he had only half of a relationship. Half of any relationship is receiving. The other half is giving. Until the two are joined, there can be no loving relationship. This was Adam and Eve's downfall. God gave them everything they could desire. (Read Genesis 2 again.) He then asked for one thing in return; he asked that they not eat of one tree in the Garden. It was a test. Would they deny this one small thing for him. Would they love him in return by giving obedience to him or would they refuse to set up the full circle of true relationships.

who do you look like?

Satan's half-circle of getting only, and not giving, made him unfit for heaven. God excluded him, and approximately one third of the angels who followed him, from heaven. These fallen angels became the demons. They are parasites, sucking out everything they can and giving nothing in return. All criminals, thieves, robbers, and murderers follow in their line. People who are only interested in what they can get, and not in what they can give back of equal value, are parasites, sucking life out of all they contact. When God created Adam, he placed him over all his creation so that Adam could give to everything in creation by ruling over it. Rulers are to rule for the welfare of those under them. They are to represent the highest form of giving to others. Adam was supposed to give to all creation. *Then God blessed them and said, "Be fruitful and multiply. Fill the earth and govern it. Reign over the fish of the sea, the birds in the sky, and all the animals that scurry along the ground"* (Genesis 1:28)

When God saw that Adam was all alone, he decided to make a partner for him, and he created Eve. He intended that the two of them would give to and receive from each other. Eve was created to give to Adam, and Adam was expected to give to Eve. While equal, man and woman are different. Each gives unique gifts to the other, and receives unique gifts back in return. In Adam and Eve's giving and receiving, a full circle would be set up which would be a loving union, resembling the union that the Triune God has within himself.

God also expected that in return for all that he had given to Adam and Eve, they would also give back to him. He created them not only to give and receive with nature and with each other, but most of all, to give and receive in their relationship with him. The gift that God asked them to give him was obedience. He told them not to eat of the tree of the knowledge of good and evil.

Satan tempted Adam and Eve by telling them that they should GET the fruit of the forbidden tree and forget about giving God anything. He tempted them to believe the half- circle lie, namely that all we need to be concerned about is what we can get for ourselves. When people think only about getting, they eventually destroy not only every-

who do you look like?

one around them, but also their relationship with nature and their relationship with God. Half-circle people, people who think only of what they can get and never what they can give, are spiritually dead people.

Adam and Eve made getting for themselves the most important desire in their lives. No longer did they live to give, or have waters of love and concern for others flow from them. Now the streams of God's love would flow only one way, into them. They changed the direction of their lives.

When Paul said, *I have been crucified with Christ and I no longer live, but Christ lives in me* (Galatians 2:20) (NIV), he meant that the inward flow, the selfish grasping, the living to get from others, died. The half-circle of merely getting was gone. The principle of having everything flowing into him died. He now lived his life based on a new principle, the full-circle of both giving and receiving. Since Christ lived in him, he could now receive and give to God as he was created to do. He was full of Jesus Christ. This fullness gave him infinite resources. The principle of having constantly to get, without giving back something of equal value, was gone. It died.

THE DIRECTION OF LOVE

I want to state it again: a disciple of Jesus can give, because he is so full of Christ that he has infinite resources in Jesus, which enable him to give. When Christ lives in us, He fills us with himself. He is without limits. His love has no limit. His power has no limit. His wealth and resources have no limit. We find that everything we ever want or need is in the One who now lives in us. Thus, Christ can transform us to be people who know the joy of giving. What joy exists when we are both giving and receiving as God created us to do! This is heaven!

Reflect

1. How is the Triune God—Father, Son, and Holy Spirit—the ultimate picture of giving and receiving?

2. What is meant when we say that Satan became a half-circle?

3. Read Genesis 1 and 2. How did God show the true relationship of giving and receiving in dealing with Adam and Eve? What commands did God give to Adam and Eve, so that their direction would be like his?

who do you look like?

4. How is conversion a change in the direction of your life?

Prayer

> *Savior, grant that we may rejoice in how much we give. Grant that we may enjoy having the rivers of your life-giving water flow from within us to bring life to all around us. Free us from being only a half-circle, concerned only about what others give to us. May we graciously receive and enjoy your gifts and others' gifts, as well. In return, may we give back to you and to them. For your sake, we pray. Amen.*

Chapter Thirty-Five

The Miraculous Increase of Love

Whoever believes in me, as the Scripture says, from within him shall flow rivers.… John 7:38

Jesus promises that all who believe in him will have not just one river flowing from them, but many rivers of love flowing from within them. Love flows out in many forms. In other words, even though we may think our lives are small and insignificant, God will grant a marvelous increase beyond anything we can imagine. I think of a very poor group of Christians in northern India who live on about $2.00 a day. Every time they make a meal, they save a handful of rice for Jesus. Every week they bring their rice to church, as a love offering. They collect and sell or give to the poor, 5,500 tons of rice each year.

who do you look like?

Two rivers of love are started by this rice. The first river consists of giving some of it to the very poor people who are living in the area of their churches. The second stream consists of selling the rest of the rice to finance 1,500 missionaries who are bringing the love of Christ to hundreds of thousands of others throughout all of India. The multiplication of the streams of love flowing out over all of India boggles the mind, especially when you realize that they start with the love of people who are living on only $2.00 per day!

As we near the end of our meditations, recall Ezekiel's vision of this mysterious increase. It is found in Ezekiel 47. The stream flowing from the temple increases in depth and intensity as Ezekiel measures it. First it is only ankle deep; then it expands to knee deep; and then waist deep; and finally it grows to be too wide to wade across. This is a picture of the life of every believer. When we become origins of rivers of love, God does things through us that are far beyond our comprehension. Not only does the stream increase, but the results are abundant. Among the many results are these:

THE MIRACULOUS INCREASE OF LOVE

Swarms of living creatures will live wherever the river flows (Ezekiel 47:9). In other words, all kinds of life will spring up because of the river.

There will be large numbers of fish, because this water flows there... (Ezekiel 47:9). Where there were no fish, now huge schools of fish swim. Where no life existed, life will spring up.

Fishermen will stand along the shore (Ezekiel 47:10). The river produces more than life and fish; it blesses the fishermen with abundant catches. Love transforms life into abundant life.

Fruit trees of all kinds will grow on both banks of the river (Ezekiel 47:12).

Their leaves will not wither ... (Ezekiel 47:12).

...nor will their fruit fail. Every month they will bear ... (Ezekiel 47:12).

Their fruit will serve for food... (Ezekiel 47:12).

...and their leaves for healing (Ezekiel 47:12).

Ezekiel mentions eight abundant results, of the rivers of life:
- Swarms of living creatures,
- Abundance of fish,
- Food for fishermen,

who do you look like?

- Fruit trees of all kinds,
- Non dying leaves,
- Constant monthly harvests of fruit,
- Food from the fruit, and
- Healing from the leaves.

God is picturing for us what will happen when the rivers of love flow from our lives. We cannot even imagine all that he will do through us.

I was visiting an orphanage in India where I met a tiny, ten-year-old girl who had gone to one of our Children's Bible Clubs and had become a believer in Jesus. (I have told her story in another book, but it fits well here as well.) She wanted to share the Bible courses with her little friends, but her teacher told her she was too young to do this, and besides that, there were no more workbooks. This news did not discourage the little girl, however, since she had memorized all the lessons!

She went out, organized her own clubs, and gave over ninety of her friends the glorious truths about Jesus. Many of these friends were transformed and taught their parents, and over fifty adults were

THE MIRACULOUS INCREASE OF LOVE

also transformed by following Jesus! A church was planted through her testimony. Someone gave Mission India one dollar, and God took that little gift of love, that little trickle of living water, and turned it into a mighty river when he used it to provide the course and teacher needed to reach the little orphan girl. The gift then began to multiply in a miraculous way, as one disciple after another was reached.

Think of what happened through a little ten-year-old orphan in just one year. Think of all the other children who were transformed. Think of their parents. Think of all the rivers of love which started to flow through each of these new disciples! Each of the other children and each parent that followed Jesus became a new source of more rivers of living water, all starting from the little girl in just one vacation period!

We never can see all the great things God is doing through our lives. When we give gifts of love and service to others, God multiplies those gifts thousands of times over, and that multiplication will continue for years and years, until Jesus comes again. Satan loves to accuse us with depressing thoughts of failure. But God doesn't think the way we think or work the way we work. Our size doesn't matter; what matters is the fact that Christ, the King of the universe dwells in us. He alone can take a little nine year old orphan and multiply her work to reach a hundred more.

God doesn't use addition; he uses multiplication of our work. When we give one tenth of all that we make each week to him, he promises that he, in turn, will open the *floodgates* of heaven and will pour out on us *blessings so great that we cannot contain them* (Malachi 3:10). Paul tells us that when we *sow generously* or *love generously*, God in turn will not only give to us generously, but he will also multiply our ability to give more and more. The more we give, the more God blesses our resources to enable us to give more (2 Corinthians 9:10). Perhaps the most wonderful of all promises is found in Ephesians 3:20, where God tells us, *Now to him who is able to do immeasurably more than all we ask or imagine…*

THE MIRACULOUS INCREASE OF LOVE

Reflect

1. Jesus tells us that more than one river will flow from us when we give. Give examples of how this has happened in the outpouring of your love.

2. Not only will the number of rivers increase when we give, but also the effects of the rivers will increase. List the eight results of Ezekiel's river as found in the devotional and explain the effects of the rivers of love that flow from us today.

3. How does feeling small and insignificant discourage us from doing anything? How does this vision correct feeling like that?

4. How do each of these verses (Malachi 3:10; 2 Corinthians 9:10, and Ephesians 3:20) show that God always multiplies the effects of our giving?

who do you look like?

Prayer

Dear Jesus, fill us to overflowing with your living waters, so that rivers of living water may flow from us to others. Show us today some of the ways in which the rivers coming from us turn into rivers flowing through others, so that we might praise you more. In your name, we pray. Amen.

Chapter Thirty-Six

Miracle Love

Whoever believes in me, as the Scripture has said, streams of living water will flow from within him.
John 7:38

An old Indian water carrier carried two leather buckets from the well to the village many times each day. One was a new leather bucket; the other bucket was old, cracked and leaky. Every morning he faithfully went to the well and filled both, and then brought the water back to the village. By the time he got to the village, however, the old bucket was only half full, since much of the water had leaked out on the way.

One day the old bucket said to the water carrier, *Why do you put up with me? Can't you see that when you get to the village, half of the water has leaked out? Why don't you buy another new bucket and save yourself some work?*

The water carrier laughed. *Old bucket, you do not know how I use you every morning, do you? Have you ever noticed all the flowers blooming along your side of the path? I water those flowers every morning with the water which leaks out of you. On the side of the new bucket, there are no flowers!*

We often feel like leaky buckets, and we think that Jesus should trade us in for someone who is more talented and more effective. The devil wants us to think that we don't amount to anything. He wants us to think that we are not valuable, that we are ugly and worthless. He tries to convince us every day that we are like that old leaky bucket. He wants us to believe that Jesus cannot use us, because we are not talented enough or don't have enough money.

But just as the water carrier used the leaks in the old bucket to water the flowers along the path, without the bucket knowing it, so Jesus uses our leaks and weaknesses in his own way. We, too, may not know how Jesus uses us. Through our weaknesses, Jesus' love can flow to others. Our weaknesses and frailties help display Jesus' power. When we are so talented, so good, and so powerful that everyone looks up to us, we get in the way of having them see Jesus' love in us. All they can see are our talents. We become the center of attention, rather than Jesus' love, which is ministering to their needs. If they cannot see Jesus in us, because they are distracted by our talents, then we cannot be used to bring the love of Jesus to them. Only when people see Jesus in us, will life flow into them. They can see Jesus best when the only explanation for what we do is that there is some supernatural love at work within us.

Selvi was an illiterate mother of four living in a slum in Chennai. She was often cheated at the marketplace, because she could not count. Her husband beat her for losing so much money, and she slipped into depression and despair.

A group of actors came to her village and performed some skits showing how important it was to learn to read and write, and Selvi, with her husband's permission, enrolled in the class. She soon

who do you look like?

learned how to read and write, but she also learned much more than that. She learned about Jesus, and Jesus came into her heart.

Rivers of living water began to flow from Selvi's life. First, she saw the importance of getting her children into school. Instead of letting them do nothing, she insisted not only that they go to school, but also that they do their work well. Her children's lives were changed for the better. More importantly, she told her family about Jesus' love and how Jesus could come to live in all of them. Selvi was transformed to become the origin of rivers of love as eternal life and love flowed from her into her husband and her children!

But it did not stop there. Many in the literacy class noticed how Selvi was changing. Earlier she had merely been sitting around her house all day, in deep depression, concerned only about herself. She did not clean the house. She did not care for her husband's nor her children's needs. But after Jesus came into her life, Selvi began to love. She learned how to sew and started a tailoring shop to supplement her husband's small income. Instead of losing money at the market by being cheated, she could now insist on the proper change. She carried herself with new dignity. She cleaned her house and insisted her children go to school. She would often say that she now had two great loves—the love of her Savior and the love of her husband.

The villagers wanted to know what had changed Selvi, so she invited them to her house to join a prayer cell. As they prayed, Jesus came into them, and Selvi encouraged them to form prayer cells in their homes. In addition to her little prayer cell, four more prayer cells were formed, and many rivers of life began to flow, transforming other families in the area. As the rivers of love flowed into the village, the entire village seemed to come to life, to new life in Jesus.

That living water of love is flowing in every nation on earth, bringing eternal life and forming new rivers of love. Some day when Jesus comes again, the earth will be transformed, and the old will pass away and new, eternal life will fill the earth.

who do you look like?

Reflect

1. Why do we sometimes feel like *leaky old buckets*?

2. Did Paul feel like a leaky bucket, according to 2 Corinthians 12:7-10? How did he get over those feelings?

3. In what ways did God use Selvi to bring new life to her village?

4. How is witnessing to others about Jesus like being a life-giver?

5. How does the picture of rivers of water flowing from us make us want to witness?

Prayer

Dear Savior, grant that this day your rivers of life may flow from us into our brothers and sisters, our parents, our uncles and aunts, and our children, so that new rivers of living water may begin to flow. Grant that all around us we may see your eternal life transforming families, villages, states, and entire nations. In your name, we pray. Amen.

Chapter Thirty-Seven
Fruit Production

Whoever believes in me, as the Scripture has said, streams of living water will flow from within him. By this he meant the Spirit, whom those who believed in him were later to receive.
John 7:38-39

But the fruit of the Spirit is love, joy peace, patience, kindness, goodness, faithfulness, gentleness and self-control.
Galatians 5:22

Ezekiel's river of love and life produced some amazing fruit trees, and these trees are a picture of what we should look like. We find some surprises about the fruit in these descriptions of fruit trees in Ezekiel. *Fruit trees of all kinds will grow on both banks of the river. Their leaves will not wither, nor will their fruit fail. Every month they will bear, because the water from the sanctuary flows to them. Their fruit will serve for food and their leaves for healing* (Ezekiel 47:12).

First, these fruit trees are surprising, because they are growing in a desert. The river is flowing through desert sand that never produced anything. God loves to transform selfish people into generous people. This is like making a fruit tree take root and grow in ground which never produced anything at all. Isaiah predicted that beautiful flowers would spring up in the desert. *The desert and the parched land will be glad; the wilderness will rejoice and blossom. Like the crocus, it will burst into bloom; it will rejoice greatly and shout for joy…Water will gush forth in the wilderness and streams in the desert* (Isaiah 35:1-2; 6) (NIV). When we depend on Christ who lives in us to produce fruit, we become like fruit-bearing trees. The fruit we bear is the different evidences of love, such as patience, kindness, gentleness. As we have seen earlier Paul gives us this list of fruit: *But when the Holy Spirit controls our lives, he will produce this kind of fruit in us: love, joy, peace, patience, kindness, goodness, faithfulness, gentleness and self-control* (Galatians 5:22-23).

who do you look like?

Another amazing characteristic of the trees in Ezekiel's vision is that the leaves never wither or die. When Christ brings his love into our hearts, that means we will have eternal life; his love is eternal. Christ's love never withers or dies. It grows within us and blossoms on the outside in glorious, attractive flowers of love, and it carries us through death into eternity.

The trees in Ezekiel's vision not only produce fruit continually, and their leaves don't wither, but they also bring healing. The fruit of patience, gentleness, kindness and compassion heal wounds in others. The love that flows from us heals the hurts, the disappointments, and the discouragements of others.

The final point, the most amazing characteristic, is that these trees bear a continual harvest. They don't produce fruit just once a year, but they produce fruit month by month. Christ in us shows himself continuously, not just at Christmas! We are to lift up the shades of selfishness and let the light of Christ's love flow from our eyes, our mouths, our ears, our hands and from everything about us; we are to keep the shades up constantly.

FRUIT PRODUCTION

John, the writer of the last book of the Bible, Revelation, was very familiar with Ezekiel's vision, and it formed much of the vision which he saw. He described heaven as having not only these kinds of trees, but also as having a crystal river flowing from the throne of God right down through the middle of Paradise, the new city of God. Trees stood on each side of the street. *And the angel showed me a pure river with the water of life, clear as crystal, flowing from the throne of God and of the Lamb, coursing down the center of main-street. On each side of the river great a tree of life, bearing twelve crops of fruit, with a fresh crop each month. The leaves were used for medicine to heal the nations. No longer will anything be cursed, for the throne of God and of the Lamb will be there, and his servants will worship him. And they will see his face, and his name will be written on their foreheads. And there will be no night there-no need for lamps or sun- for the Lord God will shine on them. And the will reign forever and ever. (Revelation 22:1-5)*

Many years ago I reviewed a large Children's Bible Club program in Hyderabad. Although there were about three hundred boys and girls in front

who do you look like?

of me, three suspicious-looking boys standing in the back, caught my eye. You could see their eyes sparkle with mischief. I asked the director who they were. He told me they were marble players who skipped school every day to gamble by playing marbles. He said that they were very bad, causing trouble at school, beating up their siblings, and being disobedient to their parents.

Jesus came into their hearts during the Children's Bible Club, and they were transformed. Filled with his Holy Spirit, they began to love as they had never loved. They became model students in school. They showed new love and respect for their parents and consideration for their siblings. They stopped living for themselves and became rivers of love and giving. As they touched others, their fruit of love brought eternal life and healing to many.

In an After School Club which Mission India sponsors (a daily club along with the ten-day Children's Bible Clubs during vacation), I interviewed a mother who obviously was not a follower of Jesus but was letting her son come to the club each day. When I asked her why she gave permission for her

FRUIT PRODUCTION

son to come, she said that he came to learn about Jesus so that he could teach the family about the love of Jesus. She said that he had become so loving, so kind, and so caring that they could hardly believe the wonderful changes. The little boy had become part of the body of Christ, showing the love of the Jesus who lived in him. That love was flowing out of him like a river and was touching and transforming his family and his neighbors.

What about it? Have you learned to look at yourself in a new way? Have you learned to STOP looking at your failures? The past is gone. The new is here. If you trust Jesus, you have opened the door to have him come into your heart. You now have a new, wonderful, eternal purpose for living. From within you, rivers of love have started to flow, transforming others. They see Christ's love in you. You are refreshingly different than the selfish, greedy world that surrounds you. You now have a completely new purpose for living!

We are children of the King of Kings, the dwelling places of the Most High God. Jesus lives in us! *I have been crucified with Christ and I no longer live, but Christ lives in me* (Galatians 2:20)!

Reflect

1. What are some of the characteristics of the fruit of love which we bear? (See the first paragraph of this chapter.)

2. What are the fruits of the spirit, according to Galatians 5:22 as quoted in this chapter?

Prayer

> *Precious Savior, we praise you for the wonder of salvation. We marvel that you can come into our spirit through your Holy Spirit, make us to be new creations of love, and grant us life forever, even after our bodies die. Grant us the power to stem the tide of selfishness to allow the rivers of your love to stream out of our lives to bless others with new life in you. In your name, we pray. Amen.*